ShawnSmallStories.com
Copyright © 2017 by Shawn Small
All rights reserved.

All rights reserved. Except as permitted under the U.S. Copyright Act of 1976, no part of this publication may be reproduced, distributed, or transmitted in any form or by any means, or stored in a database or retrieval system, without the prior written permission of the publisher.

NIV
Holy Bible, New International Version®, NIV® Copyright ©1973, 1978, 1984, 2011 by Biblica, Inc.® Used by permission. All rights reserved worldwide.

NLT
Scripture quotations are taken from the Holy Bible, New Living Translation, copyright ©1996, 2004, 2007, 2013, 2015 by Tyndale House Foundation. Used by permission of Tyndale House Publishers, Inc., Carol Stream, Illinois 60188. All rights reserved.

ESV
Scripture quotations are from the ESV® Bible (The Holy Bible, English Standard Version®), copyright © 2001 by Crossway, a publishing ministry of Good News Publishers. Used by permission. All rights reserved.

NASB
Scripture quotations taken from the New American Standard Bible® (NASB), Copyright © 1960, 1962, 1963, 1968, 1971, 1972, 1973, 1975, 1977, 1995 by The Lockman Foundation. Used by permission. www.Lockman.org

Knox
Scripture quotations taken from the Knox Bible copyright 2012 by the Archdiocese of Westminster.

NET
Scripture quoted by permission. Quotations designated (NET) are from the NET Bible® copyright ©1996-2016 by Biblical Studies Press, L.L.C. http://netbible.org. All rights reserved.

Names of some individuals have been changed to protect their privacy.

Library of Congress Control Number: 2017905362

ISBN: 978-0-9971017-3-7   *paperback*
         978-0-9971017-4-4   *ebook*

HISPUBLISHING
GROUP

Division of Human Improvement Specialists, llc.

WWW.HISPUBG.COM | *info@hispubg.com*

**THE UNLIKELY STORY OF
AN UNCOMMON COMMUNITY**

AN TOBAR NUA

~~~~~~~~

THE NEW WELL

SHAWN SMALL

Contents

An Invitation   1

    Chapter 1. Elementary School Atheist   3

    Chapter 2. The Man in Question   15

    Chapter 3. The Hound of Heaven   27

    Chapter 4. A Living Sacrifice   39

    Chapter 5. Decisions   51

    Chapter 6. Walking on the Waves   63

    Chapter 7. Foundations   75

    Chapter 8. An Tobar Nua   101

    Chapter 9. Momentum   117

    Chapter 10. A Good Harvest   131

    Chapter 11. Monumental Shifts   143

    Chapter 12. Back to Egypt   153

    In Conclusion …but Not the End   163

Afterword   171

> *Then Moses said to him,*
> *"If your Presence does not go with us,*
> *do not send us up from here."*
> Exodus 33:15 (NIV)

> *"I cannot get the way of Christ's love.*
> *Had I known what He was keeping for me,*
> *I should never have been so faint-hearted."*
> —Samuel Rutherford

An Invitation

WHEN GOD DECIDED TO WRITE A Book, He used the most effective method possible to deliver His supernatural inspired and inspiring content—through the life stories of people just like you and me. Not through long chapters of mere concepts, facts, and directives, but rather through the stories of the lives of individuals, couples, families, tribes, nations, and even the entire human race. Truth communicates powerfully through stories of God's Hand in our lives.

Nothing offers more impact than stories of God's actions and love in our daily lives. Nothing inspires us more than the honest and transparent story of people seeking to follow the Lord's leading—through all of the mountain tops, dark valleys, box canyons, seemingly unending deserts—but all eventually leading to exhilarating victories that last for eternity.

As I read the *An Tobar Nua* story I found myself humbled, challenged, and deeply encouraged by the amazing story of two overcoming fellow-believers. How I admired our God even more than ever as I read how He pursued Kelly and Susan as the "Hound of Heaven" so they could achieve a "great exploit" for Him through a most unique pilgrimage. Indeed, the story reads like Acts 29, the continuing narrative of how our Mighty God works in and then through His Children to do the impossible. As the Holy Writ states, "With God, all things are possible!"

As friends with Kelly and Susan for more than thirty years, Darlene and I cannot recommend their life story strongly enough to you.

Every struggle, every miracle, every test, every victory, every despairing complexity, every soaring victory will resonate with your heart as well. You will find yourself identifying with them time after time. Not just identifying with them, but finding heart solace, soul strength, and spirit faith scattered throughout its pages.

This couple and their wonderful family stands out as some of our favorite "overcomers" among our many friends across the world. God honored them by calling them from a life of considerable human achievement and success to an extremely challenging mission in a far-away land—to innovate a new model of ministry in a very complex environment in Ireland.

As you travel with them through their spiritual adventure, you'll learn invaluable Biblical lessons for your walk of faith. You'll strengthen in the inner man as you struggle to uncover God's hidden footsteps when nothing seems possible. Not until your back is against the wall and your faith challenged to the breaking point will God then step in and the walls crumble and fall down. The God of Jericho lives on. Mighty faith only flourishes amidst mighty tests of faith. The many lessons of leadership and governance that Kelly and Susan learned in their business and ministry life now bring valuable clarity, wisdom, and vision to us as we seek to reach all the nations of the world with God's Word.

So, no matter if you are pursuing wisdom, encouragement, or direction in your personal and professional life as you seek to maximize your life for God, you will find great benefit from this priceless story of God in action! All from our good friends, Kelly and Susan Curry, via Ireland to your doorstep.

—Dr. Bruce Wilkinson, Chairman of *Teach Every Nation*,
The New York Times best selling author of *The Prayer of Jabez*

Chapter 1

Elementary School Atheist

*A fool says in his heart
"There is no God."*
Psalm 14:1 (NIV)

*He has made everything beautiful in its time.
He has also set eternity in the human heart,
yet no one can fathom what God has done from beginning to end.*
Ecclesiastes 3:11 (NIV)

IN A QUIET SECTION OF GALWAY, Ireland, there is a quaint café tucked alongside one of the many picturesque canals. If you, like many others throughout the years, feel that invisible tug to enter the café, then you will most likely be drawn to sit near the south windows. These windows, facing the running water of the canal, are a constant moving portrait, like the view from a slow-moving boat.

The café, An Tobar Nua, may, at first, seem like nothing more than a cool little coffee shop. But as you sip on a cup of Irish tea and nibble on a warm scone you will soon notice a few unspoken subtleties. An Tobar Nua feels the way home should feel: safe, inviting, and overflowing with peace.

Keep watching and you will soon realize that the servers at the place are not simply there to provide just a hot meal or a cool drink. The staff knows many of the customers and they treat them as family. Observe long enough and you might see the barista taking time to listen to a teenager with a broken heart or the café manager counseling a young woman who recently found herself pregnant and alone. Watch a little longer and you will soon realize that this small quaint café not only serves some of the best food and desserts in Galway, it serves God's love and a message of hope. You will probably think to yourself, "What is this place, and why does it feel like home?"

To answer that question one has to understand the story of An Tobar Nua. And to do that you must travel back to 1955, the year its founders, Kelly and Susan Curry, were born. Though this story is not exclusively about their lives, they are its genesis.

～

Susan Miller grew up in the small town of Owensboro, Kentucky. Like many families in her neighborhood, Susan's blue-collar middle class family was her primary source of strength and joy. Somewhat of a tomboy, Susan was the second-born of five girls. Her early years were centered in the local Methodist church. That meant that potluck suppers, Sunday sermons, and vacation Bible schools were a foundational part of her life. Sadly, her idyllic childhood ended years before 'happily ever after.'

When Susan was fifteen, her close-knit family was devastated when her father, James, unexpectedly died of an aneurism. In the aftermath of his death, the Miller girls and their mother, Betty, numbly tried to move forward without the man they dearly loved. For Susan, quiet questions about God's seeming indifference to her family's pain began to overwhelm her.

Just across the little town a different story was unfolding.

～

The Currys' family dynamic was complex. Kelly was the youngest of three by eight years. Because of the age difference, as a child, he did not have a lot in common with his older siblings. Kelly's mother, Martha, a quiet and tender woman, was the primary source of Kelly's security. His relationship with his father, Bob, was quite different.

As a child of the Great Depression, Kelly's father, at the age of twelve, had to leave home. Living in the YMCA, he supported himself by digging postholes for twenty-five cents a day. The loss of his own father as a young child deeply affected his ability to show affection. A hard-hitting tour of duty in the Pacific during WWII toughened the already hard exterior that he exhibited to most of the world. Although these trials helped develop Kelly's father into a hardworking and brilliant man, they also left scars that would, in turn, have an effect on his family.

Although Kelly's father loved his wife and children and provided well for them, showing tenderness toward his family was difficult for him. Thus he modeled his own experiences and the lack of paternal involvement he had as a child. Statements that his father would often say, like "How much does it cost?" or "You don't know what real life is like," became an irritant to young Kelly's ears.

Though raised in the Catholic Church, by ten years old, Kelly began questioning the existence of God. During a schoolyard conversation with a fellow 4th grade classmate he pondered aloud, "If there is a god, why is there so much death and sadness in the world? If god is so good, why does he allow all of this bad stuff to happen to good people?" When no one, including adults, could answer his questions, Kelly abandoned his belief in a God and an elementary school atheist was born. How did a young boy become a skeptic at such a young age?

Even though family dynamics had an effect on Kelly's development, it was the boy's headstrong independence and his refusal to believe in a need for God that framed the majority of his choices. Father and son discussions frequently erupted into caustic arguments. They butted heads on everything imaginable and seldom agreed on anything. To let off the steam of his mounting teenage angst Kelly was drinking any alcohol he and his friends could secretly snatch.

Kelly's lack of motivation and taxing rebellion caused many of their arguments, which often ended with his father yelling in exasperation, "Kelly, you'll never amount to anything!" For most children

Kelly's age, words that potent would have broken their spirit. But Kelly was a different type of kid. Instead of crumbling under his father's criticism, he used his father's words of frustration to fuel the fire of personal achievement.

Kelly recalled one particular moment, shortly after graduating from high school, when his father tried to encourage him to make wise life choices. By this point, it was far too late for the unconnected son to accept advice from his father. This rare moment of fatherly tenderness was lost on a stubborn hard-headed young man who had, long ago, determined that his father's words were worthless. All Kelly had for his father's attempt at support was a mocking retort.

His father exploded back in anger, "If you had any brains at all you would go to college, get a degree in accounting, become a CPA, and move to Ft. Myers, Florida!"

Today, Kelly laughs when he recalls his angry response: "I will never work behind some desk or wear a tie like an office monkey. And by the way, I HATE math!" Although father and son were irreconcilable, Kelly was much more like his father than he could ever admit.

~

The first time Susan saw Kelly on campus, he was sporting a ponytail. Though they lived only a few miles away from each other as children, Susan and Kelly did not meet until college. Both had picked the University of Kentucky as their school of choice. Susan focused on education, specifically for children with special needs. Kelly, who had obtained a full scholarship through Junior Achievement, decided that a degree in political science sparked his curiosity. Much of this interest was spawned by Kelly's love for arguments and debate. He had swiftly obtained the reputation of an anti-authority wild child. But during Kelly's first week at college he entered into a debate that was far from what he was prepared to meet.

His original roommate had dropped out leaving an open bed in Kelly's dorm room. The hardened atheist did not care who moved in with him as long as the person was not one of those "Bible-thumping, Jesus-loving Christians." Kelly knew he could tolerate any lifestyle except those "crazy Christ followers."

Kelly was blasting a Bob Dylan album and was mid-pull with a Schlitz Malt Liquor when he heard his new roommate unlock the door to his dorm room. Here was the young man who would share Kelly's small living space for the next several months. In his right hand he was holding a Bible as thick as a leather-bound Webster's Dictionary, and in his left he held a framed picture of a serene Jesus Christ. Smiling a toothy grin, he turned to Kelly. "Hi, my name is Michael."

"We're going to have trouble," was the only response Kelly could muster.

Kelly's atheism energized Michael's evangelical zeal to win for Christ this sin-burdened non-believer who lived within an arm's length. Every morning, Michael would roll out of bed onto his knees and pray aloud, asking the Lord to heal Kelly's defiance and to save Kelly's soul. "Lord, I know you answer prayers. I know you love us. I know you love Kelly. Help heal his rebellious and hard heart. He is running away from you so fast. Don't let him die and go to hell..." The prayer would continue for as long as Michael saw fit.

Michael's prayers would not have been a problem for Kelly if he had not been lying three feet away trying to muffle his ears with a pillow. To combat Michael's appeals, Kelly threw impromptu parties in their dorm room. If Michael was trying to create a saint, Kelly would give him a sinner. But the more Kelly opened his room for partying, the harder, louder, and longer Michael's morning prayers grew. Half way through the fall semester, their stalemate finally came to an end one morning with peace treaty terms set by Kelly.

"Michael, if you promise to pray silently I will stop all the partying in our dorm room. What do you say? Is it a deal?"

Stopping and staring at Kelly, Michael slowly fell to his knees next to his bed. "Lord, you just heard what Kelly asked me. What do you want me to do? Do I stop praying aloud? What do you want me to do?"

Kelly stood impatiently, like a naughty child waiting to enter the principal's office.

Michael finally stood up and told Kelly, "God says that's okay." Kelly was so happy he had to restrain himself from yelling, "Praise the Lord."

—

The rest of his first semester was fairly quiet, but Michael's crusade for Kelly's soul took a different form. Through Michael's inspiration, Kelly became a magnet for all of the aggressive evangelical Christians on campus as a desired quarry on their hunt for those in need of salvation. Several times over the next few months, campus evangelists knocked on the door of this hostile atheist. They were ready for a debate that would surely sway his soul from the fires of hell.

Kelly had been an ardent reader during his teenage years. In high school, he often camped in the school library absorbing as much history, philosophy, and religious theory as he could get his hands on. Because of how well-read Kelly had become, all of these doorstep evangelists found themselves flustered by his unassailable rhetorical skills. From his viewpoint, Kelly never lost a debate even if he had to emotionally wear his opponent down to win.

Kelly always gave the same deathblow to their 'Christian' arguments. In a tone filled with skeptical arrogance, he would eventually ask, "Have you ever read the whole Bible? Do you even know what it says? If it's so important then why haven't you read it?"

In most cases, the answer remained the same. They had not exactly read the whole Bible and often did not know much of what it said. Kelly would stare at them until they left in stunned silence.

It was a little hard for a man who appreciated history and a fiery debate to take any argument about the existence of God critically when the opposing 'Christian' debater did not take the subject they were fighting for seriously enough to understand the heart of their argument. They did not know the source material that their entire premise was built upon. That lack of Biblical knowledge in the people of God stuck with Kelly for years.

―

But his pastime of debating Christians paled in interest when it came to Susan. Kelly decided to pursue Susan the minute he saw her. Even though it was doubtful that the longhaired hippy would ever pass in her conservative southern world, he asked her out several times. Her answer to his pursuits was always, "No, thank you." Eventually, the tenacity at the core of Kelly's nature broke her down. By the beginning of their sophomore year, they were a couple.

―

The first year of college had been academically rough for Kelly largely because of his loathing for authority. His poor grades in his freshman year placed Kelly on academic probation, and he lost his scholarship. Kelly moved back home for the summer. Seeing the possibility of his son squandering his future, Kelly's father decided that a few months of digging ditches and painting oil wells might straighten his son up and give him a clearer perspective. That summer, Kelly toiled physically harder than he had ever worked in his life. By the time September of his sophomore year approached, the future possibility of a life of manual labor became a powerful stimulus for Kelly. The loss of his full scholarship shook him. He knew he needed a good education to pursue the dollar bills that danced in his mind's view of the future. He knew he had to change.

By the time Kelly entered his second year of college, his love for political argument had been deflated. Part of Kelly's academic trouble came from the bad grades he earned primarily because he argued with his professors about *everything*. His strong and stubborn opinions did not play well in class. That's when the idea of a career in accounting caught his eye. As an accountant you did not argue theory. Accounting was precise—either it was right or wrong. When times were good, people needed accountants, and when times were bad, they needed them more.

Kelly also calculated the reality of becoming rich with a political science degree. Political majors were never going to become wealthy because a substantial 401K was not in that future. Accounting could meet his goals much more efficiently.

―

As Kelly planned his financial outlook, Susan was taking a very different journey. She entered into college full of stifled anger and despair. The loss of her father was the source of her indifference to God. She still put on a Christian exterior, yet it was fading on the inside. She attended church when she was at home and acted the part around her family, but she had no honest trust in God. All the while, something had been happening in her family that caused Susan to reexamine the faith of her youth.

For years, her mother reeled from the tragic loss of her husband. Struggling to raise five girls on her own had put her in a place of desperation, clinging to a deeper reliance on God. While Susan was away at university, her mother was discovering that God's promise in the Psalms was true: God is in his holy Temple. He is a father of orphans, and he defends the widows. (Psalm 68:5 CEV). In the midst of her pain, God became a husband to her broken soul.

Throughout college, Susan's skepticism and coldness toward God kept her in internal turmoil. A part of her was angry and railed at God. The other part of her wanted desperately to believe.

At one point, Susan broke off her relationship with Kelly because of his lack of faith, demonstrating her depth of spiritual confusion. Depression was always lurking in the back of her mind. Yet, watching her mother all these years, she knew there was a better way. Someone was waiting for her and she longed for Him but her pain kept her from saying, "I need You."

Kelly remained persistent in pursuing the relationship. For months, Susan did not budge, but when Kelly wanted something, nothing held him back. Exasperated, Susan finally threw all her cards on the table.

"Kelly, I'll get back together with you but I want you to come to church with me," she asserted, unsure if he'd agree to this demand.

Staring into his eyes, she watched his accounting brain carefully weigh the investment versus the loss. He was not taking her demand lightly.

"Fine. I'll go," he said.

Susan had to admit to herself that there was no one like Kelly. If he was willing to empty himself of his pride and if the God-hater would enter God's house, then she would take the risk.

By January of 1977, their final semester at the University of Kentucky, Kelly and Susan were, once again, a couple. And by that spring they were engaged.

Little did Kelly and Susan realize that a Hound was hunting them down.

Chapter 2

The Man in Question

But if from there you seek the LORD your God, you will find him if you seek him with all your heart and with all your soul.
Deuteronomy 4:29 (NIV)

And what do you benefit if you gain the whole world but lose your own soul? Is anything worth more than your soul?
Matthew 16:26 (NLT)

IN THE SUMMER OF 1977, TWO months after graduating college, Kelly and Susan were married. Susan had earned a degree in Special Education/Learning Disabilities while Kelly had completed his accounting degree. The day after he graduated, Kelly began feverishly studying for his November CPA exam. He secured a job with a large accounting firm in Louisville, Kentucky. Moving up the corporate ladder and cramming for the CPA exam left little time for Kelly to focus on his new marriage.

Their first year of marriage was not as Susan had hoped. Kelly pursued his desire for financial success while Susan taught at a local elementary school. Kelly's promise to visit church ended shortly after the 'I do's.

Looking for some sort of community life, Susan visited the local church by herself. She filled out a card checking the box that said she desired a home visit to learn more about the church. Unfortunately, the church's welcome team showed up while Susan was out and Kelly was home studying for his CPA exam. Answering the door, he impatiently listened to the parishioners' brief welcome to the community. When he had enough, Kelly cut them off.

"Did I call you to come here? I know I didn't call you. So why are we still talking?"

Shutting the door in their faces, Kelly went back to the books.

As Susan continued to rediscover the faith of her youth, tension in the marriage intensified. The new wife's ill-placed hope that Kelly would change after they were married was evaporating.

Susan realized that if her mother could find peace in the midst of her devastating loss, there was hope for her to find that same peace. But with that also came the recognition that she was utterly unable to do that in her own strength. Admitting her hopelessness was the first step back toward the loving arms of God. For the first time since she was 15, Susan opened her heart to hope and she came alive with resurrection. Within a few days, Susan was filled with a spiritual strength she had never known. The same Jesus that had hung on the cross for her was alive. Over time, Susan found her deepest longings fulfilled and her hardest questions answered in the person of Jesus Christ.

But the closer Susan grew to God, the more alienated she became from Kelly. Small differences became deep gulfs of misunderstanding between the couple. One such contentious dispute occurred when Kelly found out that Susan gave some of her own earnings in a church offering plate. He was livid. "That is the biggest waste of money I have ever heard of," he declared. "If God needs money, let him get a job. We're not giving any more money to churches."

Susan's tears over their disagreements did not sway Kelly's attitude. The more she cried, the more his frustration escalated. "Susan, believing in Jesus is like believing in a cartoon character. Face it—you live, you work, you die, you rot. There is no Jesus to save you."

But as much as Kelly tried to discourage her faith in Christ, Susan continued to cry out for God to be close to her heart. Raw faith kept her moving forward even while tension continued to soar in their marriage. But a mounting implosion was brewing.

To cope with the friction, Kelly grew numb to Susan's religious leanings. As long as her faith did not interfere with his career aspirations, there was relative harmony between them. In his mind, he was a first-rate husband, an excellent provider and a savvy businessman. They could have anything they wanted: a nice house, expensive cars, and material security. In a world where success is measured by the stuff you collect, the Currys were doing well. But Kelly was baffled as to why his wife remained discontented. Why did Susan seek some invisible benevolent being when all her visible needs were met abundantly by him?

No matter how miserable they both might have become, they stayed married for very different reasons. Susan was committed to the marriage through God's promise to her to bring her household to Christ. Kelly was determined, simply out of stubbornness, not to walk away from the marriage.

For the next several years, Kelly raced through the corporate maze and built his career by moving from a good job to a better one. This gave Kelly opportunities to collect the accolades and dollars he sought. But his golden path was abruptly frozen two years into his new job. Kelly discovered a significant case of company fraud that could potentially cause business issues. Though some suggested he remain silent, Kelly's sense of honesty motivated him to expose the scandal.

His decision had personal consequences. Kelly knew that what he had done was the right thing, but he also realized there was little or no chance for him to advance up the company ladder. Kelly was furious with those involved in the fraud issue for the personal difficulty they had imposed into his career. Abiding by the law and exposing the company corruption was ruining his life. Although the anger in his heart was real, his fears about his career were not.

Deciding it was time for a job change, Kelly accepted a position with a company based in Ft. Myers, Florida. Although Susan did not want to leave Kentucky, she had been praying for God's will to be done in their marriage. Kelly loved the sun and a move to Florida might warm his disposition. But Susan had a secure job as a teacher that she enjoyed. Relocating meant uprooting her entire life, personally and professionally. Kelly, once again, started calculating the odds. He did not want to lose this position so he came to the bargaining table with Susan: "If you are willing to move to Florida, I promise we will go to church together." Susan agreed.

In the spring of 1982, the Currys relocated to Ft. Myers. Kelly became an internal auditor for a fledgling hospital management firm. At twenty-seven years old, his plan for success was moving along nicely.

Sitting in his new home on a sunny spring afternoon, Kelly was caught off guard with a memory long forgotten: the voice of his father, booming in his eighteen-year-old ears. "If you had any brains at all you would go to college, get a degree in accounting, become a CPA, and move to Ft. Myers, Florida!" He did not know what was more disturbing—the recollection of his father's prophecy or Kelly's response when he first heard it. "I will never work behind some desk or wear a tie like an office monkey. And, by the way, I HATE math!" The irony of the memory was unnerving.

―

Five years into their marriage, Susan's faith continued to flourish. She wanted, more than anything, for Kelly to experience her enthusiasm. In Kelly's mind, the only reason someone would become a Christian was because they could not make it on their own in the real world. They needed a 'higher power' to fill in the sad little gaps of their lives. To stay true to his promise, Kelly visited a few churches with Susan but he had no intention of staying at one. That all changed the Sunday they stepped into McGregor Baptist Church.

The minister here, Jim Holbrook, did something no other pastor had done in the churches they had previously visited. Pastor Holbrook preached from the Bible, verse by verse. For the first time in his adult life, Kelly found a man who really studied and believed the Bible. The preacher's animated and impassioned style fascinated the long-avowed atheist. He decided to visit the church again. Every week, Kelly was drawn in by sermons immersed in the Bible. Of course, many of the sermons got under Kelly's skin. He was irritated by messages on tithing, dying to self, and laying one's life down for others. But the one thing Kelly could not argue was that this preacher man was not spouting religious philosophy. Pastor Holbrook believed what he was teaching and it seemed consistent with the Bible even if Kelly disagreed.

One Sunday, after church, Kelly and Susan agreed to make McGregor their church home. Over the next few months, Susan became involved in various programs at the church. Kelly continued to visit on Sundays, carefully scrutinizing all he heard. Though she had no idea what Kelly was thinking, Susan became at ease with his pew-side presence. At least he was in church.

In his book *Surprised by Joy*, C.S. Lewis wrote: "A young atheist cannot guard his faith too carefully. Dangers lie in wait on every side." If that is true, then Easter is the most dangerous time for an enquiring unbeliever to attend a vibrant church.

It was Easter of 1982 and the title of Pastor Holbrook's sermon was *The Case Any Lawyer Would Take*. Even with an enlarged holiday congregation, Pastor Holbrook was surprisingly reserved. Instead of his normal southern preacher cadence, the pastor took on the role of a trial lawyer. For the next forty minutes, he carefully examined the Resurrection of Christ as if he were an attorney before judge and jury. Piece by piece, he presented the evidence of the Resurrection. He quoted historical sources, examined a cultural portrait of the Roman occupied Israel of Jesus day, listed the proofs for a historic, bodily resurrection of Christ. Kelly knew that the Resurrection of Christ was the crux of his whole argument against Christianity. If the Resurrection of Christ never occurred, then the entirety of Christianity was false. But if it was true...

Working in the hospital industry had presented data to Kelly that could not be ignored. Seeing people die was an everyday part of his job. But he could not discount the fact that people with faith often died differently than the agnostic or unbeliever. And families with faith dealt with loss differently than those with no belief in the afterlife. Reading the Koran, the Bhagavad Gita and the writings of Confucius in high school had been a part of Kelly's search for religious understanding. None of those religious writings ever presented anything as audacious as resurrection. As far as science was concerned, those who died in the hospital remained dead. There was no way Kelly could simply take Christ's Resurrection on faith alone.

As Kelly sat there that Easter Sunday wrestling with the multitude of information that swirled in his mind, the preacher ended his homily the most disturbing way Kelly could have imagined.

His impassioned voice rising, Pastor Holbrook spoke to a congregation on the edge of their seats and explained that God never expected us to accept the Resurrection on faith alone. He encouraged them to explore the overwhelming historical evidence with eyes of reason and logic. All other miracles presented in the Bible pale in significance to the Resurrection. Christ coming back from the dead is central to Christian belief. If Christ was crucified and never rose from the dead, then 2000 years of Christianity were in vain. But if He did rise from the dead, that singular event was the nexus of history and the primary purpose of our existence. The sermon dared Kelly to examine the evidence.

As the congregation left the sanctuary, heading home to ham dinners and Easter egg hunts, the atheist since elementary school sat confounded. Kelly's carefully crafted philosophy of the world was crumbling under his feet.

―

The challenge given by Pastor Holbrook that Easter wedged itself into Kelly's mind. He decided, once and for all, to end his doubts about the possibility of God's existence by probing the evidence of the Resurrection with an auditor's eye. He began to meticulously study the miracle of miracles. Whenever he found a source, he dove in for even deeper understanding.

Reading the Bible became a necessary part of his investigation. As with any other book, he started at the beginning, the book of Genesis. What he discovered stunned him. This book, the most read in the history of mankind, was full of sex, violence, and raw humanity. Real characters, existing with damning flaws, filled the stories in the Bible. Nothing was sugar-coated. This was a tell-all book that shared a story of sin and redemption from cover to cover. Kelly had always enjoyed acquiring information and this new source of knowledge began to awaken a hunger for truth.

Even while Kelly researched the legitimacy of the Resurrection, his overall lifestyle remained the same. He wanted to make a ton of money and his current career path made that possible. Kelly used his weekends to hobnob with clients. Golf, drinking binges, and gambling were a regular part of his career. "If I work hard then I should be able to play hard" was Kelly's motto of justification.

Susan had no idea that her husband was on a private quest for understanding. In fact, she started to lose hope that he would ever change. She knew Kelly was a good and hardworking man, but he was also obsessed with his career. Susan wanted a world shared fully with her husband; a marriage that engaged in the life God wanted for them.

Although there were other factors adding to the growing tension in their marriage, one of the greatest was the lack of children. They had tried for years, but Susan was not getting pregnant. As they grew further apart, Susan was no longer able to mask the mounting loneliness. All she could do was pray and ask God to help fill the void that was deepening in their marriage.

~

By November of 1982, Kelly began the New Testament. He entered into the pages about the life of Jesus, the Man in Question. Reading the Gospels of Matthew, Mark, and Luke left him with an enormous dilemma. At the end of each of these Gospels, there came a point where the High Priest of Israel asks a captive Jesus the question that will decide if he will live or die: "If you are the Christ, tell us."

Jesus answered, "If I tell you, you will not believe me, and if I asked you, you would not answer. But from now on, the Son of Man will be seated at the right hand of the mighty God."

They all asked, "Are you then the Son of God?"

He replied, "You are right in saying I am."

Kelly was struck with the weight of Jesus' words. Standing before his accusers, execution hanging over his head, Jesus answers the charge of being the Messiah, the Son of God with the words "I am." Jesus of Nazareth did not back down an inch but clearly proclaimed Himself God. Another piece of the puzzle fell into place. Jesus was not just a martyr or good teacher. He actually believed He was God come in the flesh to die for humanity.

~

A month later, Dr. Bruce Wilkinson, a foremost Christian teacher, spoke at the annual managers' meeting of the company where Kelly worked. At the time, the company was privately owned and the Christian owner shared his faith openly.

Bruce taught an intensive study of what Kelly had been secretly exploring the last nine months. Surveying the entire Old Testament, Bruce focused on the multitude of prophecies that pointed to a coming Messiah. Genesis through Malachi were filled with words that indicated directly that Christ was the Messiah.

Kelly had spent the last few months reading those same words in the Old Testament. The final pieces fell into place. And just like that, the debate ended. Kelly had been seeking truth but he now realized that truth was not a concept or a thing to be obtained. Truth was a person. Jesus claimed this in John 14, 'I am the way, the truth, and the life: no man comes to the Father, but by me'.

The exhausted skeptic who had fought Christianity like an atheist crusader could no longer deny the mass of data presented. The more he dug, the more the undeniable facts came to the surface. This Jesus of Nazareth, the one who came to earth claiming to be God in the flesh, who turned history upside down with His presence, who was crucified on a cross, who had been killed, and who had risen from the dead three days later—nothing else mattered.

Kelly Curry may have denied the existence of God at ten years of age but now, 18 years later, he could no longer escape the truth. As Bruce prayed, Kelly bowed his head in surrender and asked the Resurrected One to enter his life.

But even though Christ had saved Kelly's soul, capturing his heart would take much longer.

Chapter 3

The Hound of Heaven

*Therefore, he is able to save completely
those who come to God through him,
because he always lives to intercede for them.*
Hebrews 7:25 (NIV)

For nothing is impossible with God.
Luke 1:37 (NIV)

KELLY AND SUSAN WERE BAPTIZED on Easter in 1983. Significant changes in the marriage were immediate. Their emotionally tumultuous world settled down. The couple began to volunteer together at McGregor Baptist and quickly became involved in the life of the church. But something in their lives was still amiss.

Kelly steadily moved forward in his career and by 1985 he reached a vice-president position. He wondered if it was possible that his goals for financial success were synonymous with the will of God. But even as his career was flourishing, the couple's hope for children was plummeting.

They were still without a baby after eight years of marriage. All the tests showed that there were no physical conditions preventing a pregnancy. God certainly knew the desire of their hearts, yet they remained childless. Susan was beside herself.

One day, while begging God for answers to their infertility, Susan felt the need to fast. Not completely understanding the concept of fasting, but simply taking the desire as a call to obedience, Susan fasted for three days.

During that time, she came across an Old Testament story where the prophet Elisha spoke a blessing from the Lord to a woman who could not have children. About this time next year, you will have a child. (2 Kings 4:16) The words of Elisha filled her with hope. The fast ended with Susan taking those words as a promise for her life. After writing the promise down in her journal, she checked the calendar.

"If this is true for me, then I should be pregnant in the next three months."

For the first time in years, Susan believed she would be a mother.

But after three months Susan was still not pregnant. Feeling hopeless, Susan asked God why He did not listen to her prayers for a baby. How could she ever trust He'd answer her prayers? How could she ever believe His promises? Slowly Susan received an answer in her heart. The tone of the voice was gentle and full of compassion:

> *"Susan, since the day your father died, you have not trusted me. The question is not whether I love you enough to give you a baby. I love you as much now as I ever could. The question is will you trust me whether you are pregnant or not? Will you serve me regardless of whether you understand My ways?"*

Susan was broken by these words. Confronted face to face with the sovereignty of God, she yielded to the One who alone knew the beginning from the end and was all-wise, even if His ways were beyond her understanding. The grace to trust God settled deep within her as she prayed out loud, "Lord, I will follow you whether you give me a child or not. I will not turn away from You."

Kelly and Susan ended their visits to fertility doctors and started the adoption process. But on the 4th of July, 1985, while they were on one of Kelly's business trips to Key West, Susan became nauseous with the smell of fish wafting in from the harbor. It was undoubtedly morning sickness. Seven months later, Natalie was born. Another daughter, Leah, would come three years later.

Not only had God met the desires of her heart, but He had taught her how to have an unshakeable trust in the goodness of His will.

From the outside, the Currys' world looked perfect. A new baby, a successful career and a comfortable lifestyle painted a picture of the ideal American couple. But one Sunday's sermon, in the spring of 1986, proved that their perfect world was still on a shaky foundation.

Something in Pastor Holbrook's tone that Sunday caught Kelly's attention. For three years, Kelly had listened to Sunday sermons with the enthusiasm of a hungry student. But the majority of Kelly's Christianity remained theory rather than practice. He believed the words of Christ were true, but living them out consistently had not become a reality in his life.

In his booming voice, the preacher declared, "Some of you may be called out from behind your desk to minister to others." Kelly fixated on the pastor's words.

Although Pastor Holbrook's sermon was intended for recruiting church volunteers, Kelly heard something different. Kelly was stunned. He knew the words were for him. He felt that God wanted him to go into ministry.

Thoughts pummeled his brain. Kelly considered himself to be a good man. He tithed regularly to the church and even taught children's Sunday school. What more did God expect from him?

Susan had no idea of Kelly's inner turmoil during the sermon. That afternoon he confessed, "Susan, I am afraid to allow God to be Lord of my life. I don't want to end up as a missionary in a foreign land."

Unable to understand Kelly's sudden mind-boggling statement, Susan felt clueless. For the next two months, Kelly was tormented by the battle waging in his heart. He did not pray, read his Bible, go to church, watch TV, play golf or eat a sandwich without thinking about God's challenge. As far as Kelly was concerned, this nerve-racking conflict of wills (his and God's) had to end. Eventually he declared, "You're going to have to get yourself another boy, God. Ministry is not for me."

That was the end of the conversation. The Spirit was quenched as Kelly asserted his will. Kelly was, once again, the captain of his soul.

⁓

As Kelly consciously put down the Bible and ceased praying, a hollow place grew in his soul. He tried filling the void with the one thing he knew best: a dogged pursuit of business. Even more frightening? A marriage that had been healing and growing stronger was suddenly sideswiped as Kelly turned his face from God. On the outside all looked well but Kelly wore a mask. The more he dove into business, the less time he spent at home with his wife and small child. Every step forward in his career took him farther from his family.

At thirty-four, Kelly was reaching goals he had set for himself long ago. But as he became ever more ambitious, he pushed for more. Although the rewards of the corporate world seemed to validate his focus, Kelly felt a gnawing void that could not be filled.

Kelly not only worked hard, he played hard. One of his distractions started innocently. One classic Corvette to satisfy Kelly's interest turned into three. Six created a hobby and nine Corvettes made a collection. Yet no matter how much stuff he acquired, or how well he succeeded at work, Kelly remained miserable. To self-medicate, Kelly increased his drinking to try to deal with the tension that constantly clouded his heart and home.

Even as Susan became more involved in church and drew closer to the Lord, Kelly became more engrossed in work and shut out the

Lord even more. His focus on his job left Kelly less and less time to spend with his family, though he tried to convince himself that his career was beneficial to them. As Susan became less understanding about Kelly's absence, the more Kelly felt that he was misunderstood and taken for granted.

Susan encouraged Kelly to return to the Lord, but her love for God became a painful reminder of his own rejection of God's call. As Kelly emotionally pushed Susan away, their marriage suffered and communication failed. Now, along with the void, Kelly started to experience guilt and shame. One particular question weighed on his mind: How could he be successful everywhere else in his life but an utter failure in his home?

By 1992, the marriage was in a desperate state. Without the deeper spiritual connection they had once shared, the couple grew further apart. Kelly refused to talk about their failing marriage or deal with his spiritual backsliding. To both Kelly and Susan, the other mate was the primary problem in their relationship.

Unable to hide the growing difficulties, Susan eventually asked two of her friends to pray for their marriage.

She later phoned another Christian mentor and friend asking for guidance. Speaking through her despair, Susan shared her greatest fear, "I don't know if I believe anymore that God can save this marriage. I don't know that He is able." She confided that she sometimes wanted to just pick up her daughters and leave.

Her friend asked Susan a tough question. "Has God told you to leave?"

Susan reluctantly admitted, "No."

The mentor's words were weighty. "Then, Susan, if you leave, you will have to tell me why you left."

Those words of accountability helped Susan hold onto the relationship, even as she doubted the possibility of change.

But in the following days the Lord began to impress upon Susan's heart, "Susan, you work on Susan and let me be Kelly's Holy Spirit. He is in good hands."

Susan changed her prayers from, "God change Kelly" to "God, I give you Kelly; he is Yours. Change me into what I need to be for You and for him."

―

As the weeks went by, Susan's doubt continued to nag at her thoughts, but her spoken accountability to her friend kept her from making any rash decisions. One day, in a prayer meeting, she heard her pastor's wife saying she had prayed that the Hound of Heaven would chase after a family member who was running from the Lord. Her words resonated with Susan.

Believing the reference to the Hound of Heaven came out of the Bible, Susan started praying for the Hound to pursue Kelly, even in his sleep. A few days after she began her silent prayer, Kelly began to develop insomnia. For the next few months, he never got more than three straight hours of sleep a night. His lack of rest added to a 70-hour work-week started to take a toll on his health. Because of his souring mood, Kelly began to avoid any and all friends who were followers of Christ. To see Jesus in them was tormenting.

Even as Kelly seemed to grow more distant, Susan felt the Lord encourage her to pray for the fulfillment of His purpose in their marriage. She hung on to a promise in Jeremiah 29:11, "For I know the plans I have for you," declares the LORD, "plans to prosper you and not to harm you, plans to give you hope and a future." Often she would tell the Lord she could not see any future in the marriage, but then Susan would feel His encouragement and peace to keep trusting. Strangely enough, the more peaceful Susan became, the more irritable Kelly grew.

Their only visit together to a marriage counselor was a disaster. Kelly was tangled up on the inside. Irritated, Kelly expressed his view of the marriage. He believed he was an excellent provider and good father, productive in his church and community. He told the counselor that the problem was Susan's. He was dealing with "real problems in the real world" while she stayed at home with a lot of time to think about meaningless things. His closing words to the counselor as he left were, "I don't have a problem and you're wasting my time."

Moments like these discouraged Susan. At times she would turn to God and say, "You want me to pray for Your will in this marriage? Are you kidding? Do You not see that nothing is happening?"

But after Susan quieted down, she would go back to praying for the Hound of Heaven to chase down her husband. There was not another human in the world that could sway Kelly if he was not willing to stop running. She continued to feel God saying, "Be patient." The Hound was closing in on His prey.

~

One of Kelly's friends told him about an upcoming marriage conference in Virginia. Trying to bring an olive branch to the marriage and demonstrate his willingness to work on their relationship, Kelly sheepishly mentioned the conference to Susan. She was dumbfounded that he would be willing to attend a marriage conference.

A few weeks later, Kelly learned he was scheduled for a business trip to Europe and wives were invited. He had an out as he was sure that Susan would pick the trip over the conference. But Susan did not want to go on a trip to Europe with her marriage imploding, even though she knew Kelly did not want to go to Europe alone. Surprisingly, her counselor encouraged her to support her husband and see what God might do. Susan knew the marriage conference was an answer to years of prayer, but she also realized this was a moment she needed to trust God no matter how the circumstances looked. When Susan agreed to go to Europe, Kelly thought he had dodged a bullet. He would still benefit from the goodwill resulting from the mere suggestion that they attend a marriage conference, without actually having to go.

Days later, the European trip was cancelled, and Kelly realized he had run out of excuses. He would have to eat his words and go to the dreaded gathering of couples sharing their "sappy stories" of marriages more screwed up than his.

~

It was May of 1993. Kelly was livid as he sat in the packed meeting room on the first night of the conference. He seated himself on the back row, close to the door, with his arms crossed as if to say, "I dare anyone to say a word to me." As the evening speaker came to the podium and shared his own story of a marriage gone terribly wrong, Kelly thought, "This guy is a bigger jerk than me." The man openly spoke of his volatile marriage filled with anger, bitterness, and looming unresolved issues, but it was a marriage that God had healed.

Kelly thought back to years earlier when he uncovered the fraud incident at his former employer that almost ruined his career. He wondered why thoughts of revenge cropped up at that moment. He pondered all the drinking and partying he had done in the name of success. What about all the pain he had caused Susan during their fourteen years of marriage? Remembering back to how he sought her in college, he wondered what had caused him to have such a calloused heart for a woman he once adored.

But out of all of the selfish, sinful acts, the elaborate facades he created to impress others, and a life built on the quest for dollars and power, none of these compared to the day he told God "No! I will not follow You." Kelly recognized that his rejection of God was the heart of the matter.

The only fullness Kelly had ever experienced in his life was in relationship with the person of Jesus Christ. All other motivations had led to his personal misery and suffering in the lives of others. The words of C.S. Lewis explained Kelly's sudden revelation. "And there I found what appalled me; a zoo of lusts, a bedlam of ambitions, a nursery of fears, a harem of fondled hatreds. My name was legion."

The conference speaker shared out of the Gospel of Matthew about the forgiveness of Christ. Everything inside of Kelly was screaming to run out of the room and hide. But he was tired of running. The room hushed as the speaker whispered into his microphone.

"Please bow your heads and close your eyes. Is there anybody in this room that would like to rededicate their lives to Christ? Please raise your hand."

The Hound had found his prey and Kelly was too tired to escape. As he battled with bowing before the King of kings, he heard clearly from the Holy Spirit, "This is your last chance."

Susan did not realize that Kelly had slowly raised his hand. He felt like he was falling into a grave. His will was dead and gone. There was no denying the truth. His days of running were over. Kelly Curry resolved in his heart, "I give up. I'll do it Your way instead of mine." Kelly Curry was now Christ's man.

Chapter 4

A Living Sacrifice

*Does the Lord delight in burnt offerings and sacrifices
as much as in obeying the Lord?
To obey is better than sacrifice,
and to heed is better than the fat of rams.*
1 Samuel 15:22 (NIV)

*Therefore, I urge you, brothers and sisters, in view of God's mercy,
to offer your bodies as a living sacrifice, holy and
pleasing to God—this is your true and proper worship.*
Romans 12:1 (NIV)

KELLY AND SUSAN WALKED BACK TO their room that night in silence. Kelly was exhausted from the transformation of his hardened heart, and the range of emotions he was experiencing left him without words. Susan, not knowing what had happened to Kelly, read his face and assumed that he was still irritated at being at the conference. The couple climbed into bed, each unaware of what the other was thinking. Moments after his head touched the pillow, Kelly sunk into the deepest sleep he had experienced in years.

That night Kelly had a dream: *He was running and trying to hide. Sand surrounded him and he could hear the crash of the sea. Someone, or Something, was after him. The beach he was on did not give him a place to hide. He was terrified. Through the darkness of the dream, Kelly became aware of his Pursuer. An imposing angel was scanning the beach in search of his quarry and next to the angel was a massive and powerful dog, but Kelly didn't feel that it meant to harm him. Suddenly, the dog turned towards Kelly and, as if he sensed the dog's leading, the angel followed, beckoning with his hand for Kelly to come.*

Little did Susan realize that the Hound of Heaven, the Holy Spirit, was pursuing Kelly in the exact way that she had prayed. In his dreams. Kelly had been thrashing so violently in the bed that Susan woke him, thinking he was having a bad dream.

Kelly silently prayed that he would be able to go back to sleep. Several hours later, he awoke with a start. As he lay in bed with his eyes closed, Kelly's mind clearly heard the Voice of the Holy Spirit asking for him to be *filled to overflowing with His Presence*. Although Kelly heard the words, he was not sure of their meaning.

Kelly went running that morning. As he ran, something strange began to happen. Praise flowed from his lips like a life-giving deluge in the desert. Kelly returned to the hotel for a shower. Susan, brushing her teeth mere feet from Kelly, was still unaware of what was taking place in his heart. As she prepared for the morning session, she felt disheartened as she wondered why they were even wasting their time on a marriage retreat. It all seemed hopeless. A few feet away from Susan, behind the shower curtain, Kelly suddenly slumped to the floor as if struck dead.

As he lay on the floor of the shower, Kelly felt like the Holy Spirit was pulsing clear, clean water into his body like jets from the shower. The filth that had found a comfortable place in his life started to drain from his body. The stench of sin, selfishness, bitterness and deception came out of Kelly. He knew Jesus was with him. At any time, he could have said, "Stop," but for the first time in his life, Kelly Curry was clean. He was free and he was truly alive.

After the shower, Kelly sat on the bed, his head spinning from hours of relentless epiphanies. He prayed, "Lord, I need to know that this is real."

Picking up Susan's Bible, Kelly turned to the Old Testament. His eyes fell on 1 Samuel 15:22. "Does the LORD delight in burnt offerings and sacrifices as much as in obeying the LORD? To obey is better than sacrifice, and to heed is better than the fat of rams." Not understanding what he was reading, he flipped to the New Testament and the verse that caught his attention was out of Romans. "Therefore, I urge you, brothers and sisters, in view of God's mercy, to offer your bodies as a living sacrifice, holy and pleasing to God—this is your true and proper worship."

Again, Kelly prayed. "What are you saying to me God?" The answer came swiftly. "I want you to quit drinking." The words from the Holy Spirit were as plain as day. "Done," was Kelly's response.

Susan and Kelly went to the morning session. From the moment the morning worship began, the normally emotionally stagnant Kelly broke into tears. To Susan, Kelly's tears were the final sign that he was about to ask her for a divorce. Kelly still said nothing.

As they sat down for the first session of the morning, Kelly opened up the workbook provided for the retreat. The lesson for the day started with 1 Samuel 15:22 and Romans 12:1-2, the very scriptures Kelly had randomly opened to in Susan's Bible just an hour before. As the morning session came to an end, Kelly said to Susan "We need to talk. I have to tell you something."

Susan's stomach tightened as they walked back to their room. Sensing the agitation in Kelly, she expected him to say he was leaving her. Instead, he shared what had happened to him over the last twelve hours.

When he relayed his dream and described the large dog that pursued him, Susan cried out, "That's the Hound of Heaven! I've been praying for the Hound of Heaven to come after you." Both Susan and Kelly were amazed at God's faithfulness and specific answer to Susan's prayers.

Kelly later found out that *The Hound of Heaven* was a classic poem by the English poet Francis Thompson. A hound doggedly pursues its quarry. Never ceasing the chase and drawing ever closer with steady swiftness, it patiently closes in on its prey. The autobiographical poem reflected the author's own attempted escape from God's hand. The symbolism was clear: God ever pursues a soul that is fleeing His presence. Though they may try to run from the Almighty, God's unwavering persistence will one day bring the prodigal home. He is unrelenting in His pursuit. The Holy Spirit is the Hound of Heaven and His pursuit will continue until His quarry yields to His love and forgiveness.

Knowing that neither she nor Kelly could have orchestrated the dream and that God used an old English poem that neither of them had heard of, convinced Susan that the Holy Spirit was at work in a way she could not question.

On Sunday morning, at the end of the conference, they stayed for an extra session that was offered on the Holy Spirit's role in guiding the believer. They came down to the altar, hand in hand, and asked God for any gifts of grace He might give them to help them on their journey. As they began to praise God together, Kelly knew, standing at that altar with the woman he loved more than any other person in the world, that it was time for him to take responsibility for his marriage. He asked God what it was that had tormented him all of these years and held him back from total surrender to Jesus. The answer was clear: FEAR. Hearing the words of St. Matthew brought Kelly peace: But if it is by the Spirit of God that I drive out demons, then the kingdom of God has come upon you. (Matthew 12:28) Kelly was clean of his sin and ready to live out his repentance.

Susan had come to Virginia with Kelly, but she was going back to Florida with a changed man. The old Kelly was transformed, turned inside out, and now a part of a very different kingdom.

—

The next six months became a season of digging up the emotional and spiritual weeds that had taken over their marriage from day one. A fresh season of planting healthy seeds from the Word of God into their marriage brought a quick harvest. For the first time, Kelly became a spiritual leader in his home. Many in their church wondered how this man, who used to sit like a sullen teenager on Sundays, now stood in the front row raising his hands in worship. The back-row, all-out, flag-waving, card-carrying pagan was a changed man. And though delighted with the transformation, Susan still wondered if it might wear off. Trust was going to take time.

As Kelly grew in his newly restored relationship with God, he prayed for more insight into God's word. Inspired by Susan's journaling, Kelly began to record what God spoke to him out of the Scriptures, constantly striving to hear more of God's voice.

In the summer of 1993, Kelly's prayer for clarity in hearing God's voice came to pass in a way he could never have imagined. While driving home from work one evening, Kelly felt an urgency to drive to a particular church in Immokalee, Florida, which was thirty miles away. He had never been to Immokalee, but he felt the Holy Spirit telling him to talk to the pastor about Bibles, hymnals, and choir robes. He stopped and prayed. Peace came. But a week went by and Kelly had taken no action.

A few days later, as Kelly sorted through a stack of work piled on his desk, he heard the Spirit whisper in his ear. "Kelly, are you going to Immokalee?" Kelly thought aloud, "I guess if You created the world in six days You can handle the workload on my desk today." Kelly immediately left work and drove in silence, wondering what his mission might entail. When he arrived in the small town, he drove slowly, looking for a church. He came across a small church but no one was there. He prayed, "What next, Lord? Where do I go?"

The answer came quickly. "Stop here."

Kelly stopped in front of a 1920's clapboard home. An elderly man sat on the porch in a rocking chair. He watched Kelly getting out of his car with curiosity. Kelly walked up to the porch and addressed the gentleman.

"Hello, sir. There's a church around the corner but there's no one there. Do you know how I could get in touch with the pastor?"

"Sure I do," The man said with a smile. "It's closed today, but my daughter works for the church and she's inside."

Kelly wrote down the pastor's phone number. Later that day, he spoke to the pastor on the phone to arrange a Sunday morning to visit. Two weeks later Kelly arrived at the small church. The rousing service, where parishioners were dressed to the hilt and praised in bold freedom, went on for three hours. At the end of the service, Kelly walked up to the pastor and shook his hand.

"Pastor, I want to talk to you about Bibles and hymnals," Kelly started.

"Well, we definitely need Bibles and hymnals, but we're a very poor church and we can't afford to purchase anything you might be selling," the pastor said, assuming that Kelly was a salesman who had come to peddle his goods.

"Oh no, sir, you don't understand. You've been praying for Bibles and hymnals. God sent me to get them to you. How many do you need?"

The pastor started to cry. "I can't believe this. Just this morning we prayed again for Bibles and hymnals."

The two prayed together, both in awe of God's faithfulness. As Kelly got up to leave the church, he felt the Holy Spirit say to him, "Okay, Kelly. If you are not going to ask the pastor, I will have him ask you." Before Kelly turned around, the pastor spoke.

"Mr. Curry, before you leave, did God speak to you about choir robes?"

Astounded by God's specific will, Kelly said with a smile, "Well, as a matter of fact, He did."

~

Kelly was learning to hear and trust the voice of God and what it meant to walk in obedience. Over the next several months, Kelly sensed God asking him to speak words of encouragement to people in the oddest places and in the strangest ways. Kelly witnessed to strangers in the mall and handed out Bibles to construction workers while he went running. He became a witnessing fool. It did not matter if they were homeless or Wall Street bankers; Kelly was compelled to share Christ with whomever God brought across his path. When he was obedient to share, the recipients were often responsive to God's love. Kelly became radical for Christ.

One evening, Susan invited a missionary couple on furlough over for dinner. She wanted to hear their stories of ministry in the Philippines. Years ago, Kelly had assumed they were out of their minds for leaving the U.S. with their family in tow to serve a foreign people in a third world nation. But on this night, he heard their stories with different ears. He realized how courageous the couple had been for the Lord. Kelly listened eagerly as the husband encouraged him to read the Bible from cover to cover. Their conversation that night set a hunger for God's Word in both Kelly and Susan's heart and it became a core foundation for God's speaking guidance into their lives.

~

Susan continued to be confounded with Kelly's transformation. How could someone turn around so quickly? Unused to Kelly's spiritual leadership in their home, Susan also began to sense a season of change approaching in their lives and the prospect of it was making her uncomfortable. What if Kelly wasn't really hearing from God? What if Kelly suddenly went back to his old ways? What if this excitement for the Lord wore off? In addition, there was the fear that God might ask them to do something they could not handle or to go somewhere they did not want to go. What if they were called to a foreign place like her missionary friends? Susan did not feel like she could ever leave her family and friends. More than anything, she was anxious about the unknown. The guilt of questioning God, after all He had done to answer her prayers, caused Susan to do some real soul-searching.

Something happened one sunny morning in August that started to answer Susan's gnawing questions. As she quietly walked through her neighborhood, she began to pray for God's will in the life of her family. Immediately, the Lord spoke to her about being available for what He wanted them to do. She found herself standing in front of a mailbox covered in vine blossoms that snaked up the side of the post. Unexpectedly, Susan had a vision. In her mind, she saw a small thatch-roofed cottage. The stone house was covered in vine blossoms and colorful flowerbeds surrounded the cozy home. Then the vision ended. Susan was puzzled. She did not know what it had meant. Susan went home and recorded the vision in her prayer journal. As she closed her journal she heard a whisper in her spirit. "Prepare for what I have for you." Susan kept the vision to herself.

―

In October of that same year, Kelly was flying home from a business trip with an open Bible in his lap. He was reading out of Deuteronomy chapter 11:7-12. "But it was your own eyes that saw all these great things the LORD has done." This caught his attention. The transformation in Kelly's life was evidence of the great things the Lord could do. "Observe therefore all the commands I am giving you today, so that you may have the strength to go in and take over the land that you are crossing the Jordan to possess." As Kelly read the phrase *crossing the Jordan*, in his mind he heard "*crossing the Atlantic*" instead. He stopped for a moment and allowed the words to ring in his mind. "And so that you may live long in the land the Lord swore to your ancestors to give to them and their descendants, a land flowing with milk and honey." He continued reading. "The land you are entering to take over is not like the land of Egypt, from which you have come, where you planted your seed and irrigated it by foot as in a vegetable garden." But instead of Egypt, Kelly heard "*Florida*." "But the land you are crossing the Jordan (Atlantic) to take possession of is a land of mountains and valleys that drinks rain from heaven." Kelly's ancestors were long ago from Ireland. Though he knew little about the country, he did know that it was a land of mist and rain. In that moment, the will of God became crystal clear to Kelly. God wanted them to move to Ireland.

Kelly returned home that evening quite shaken. He immediately sat down with Susan and shared the word he believed God had spoken to him. Susan's thatch-roofed cottage vision from earlier that year struck her like a lightning bolt. But still wary of the trustworthiness of Kelly's transformation and his ability to hear from God, she did not share it with Kelly.

Little did they know, a daunting decision lay at their feet that would change the trajectory of their lives.

Chapter 5

Decisions

*Those who trust in the Lord are like Mount Zion,
which cannot be shaken but endures forever.
As the mountains surround Jerusalem,
so the Lord surrounds his people
both now and forevermore.*
Psalm 125:1-2 (NIV)

*Do not say to your neighbor,
"Come back tomorrow and I'll give it to you"—
when you already have it with you.*
Proverbs 3:28 (NIV)

KELLY AND SUSAN CONSIDERED A CALL to Ireland both surprising and humbling. But each of them viewed the call differently. To Kelly, the call was clear. To Susan, the call was daunting. The vision of the thatched roof cottage that seemed to tie in with Kelly's scriptural promise did not lessen the fact that he had just started listening to and obeying God. Trusting God was not as difficult after all that she had learned through the past years, but trusting Kelly to hear from God was something she struggled with as his spiritual transformation was still fresh and seemingly untested. Susan was reluctant to jump wholeheartedly without further confirmation from the Lord, and so she continued to keep her vision to herself.

As a couple, they decided they needed three things to help them understand God's will for their lives. First, they agreed they needed to pray more and ask the Lord to confirm the call. Second, they would seek counsel from people who had wisdom in the ways of God, especially in the discernment of a call. Third, they would tell no one where they thought the Lord might be calling them so as not to cloud anyone's opinion.

Almost immediately, Ireland popped up everywhere they went. It was not unusual for ordinary things to happen that reminded them of their call to the Emerald Isle—like the time they rode in an elevator that happened to be playing Irish tunes or the time they walked through a bookstore and their eyes were immediately drawn to an Irish book in a pile of a hundred other books. As they sought the Lord together, it drew the couple closer and Susan began to trust her husband with their marriage and the spiritual leadership of their family and to trust the Lord with her future.

As they sought out others in the ministry and conferred with them about their own calls from the Lord, it became clear to the Currys that their feelings were legitimate. One pastor told them, "If you feel called to do something for the Lord and say 'No', He will get someone else to do it because He will accomplish His will. But you'll never forget that you were His first choice and that you missed the blessing of obedience."

~

The Currys booked a family vacation to Europe during the summer of 1994. The plan was to visit their missionary friends in England and then take a short side trip to Ireland to at least get a glimpse of this land that was 'flowing with milk and honey that drinks rain from heaven'. In a way only God could orchestrate, the pieces of the trip amazingly fell together. The ordering of all the details showed God's favor, and the couple felt encouraged in taking this exploratory step.

In June, the family arrived in Ireland for their scouting trip. As they drove from the Shannon airport to their lodging, they passed through Adare, an old village with a quaint row of tiny cottages surrounded by stone walls and lovely gardens. Susan asked Kelly to stop so she could take a picture of the cluster of cottages. Susan was a bit shaken when she recognized one of the cottages as the one she had seen in her vision. She took a photo of the very picture God had given her months before in Florida.

They drove around the Ring of Kerry, devouring the emerald landscape and coastal mountains that dropped into churning seas. With every corner they turned on the winding roads and every small village they explored, there was a boundless joy that filled Susan and Kelly and made them feel as if they were discovering hidden treasure. But a sense of gravity tempered their wonder. Questions swirled in their minds. How would God do this thing He had called them to? What exactly was He calling them to do if they came?

On one of their mornings in Ireland, Susan read Psalm 125: "Those who trust in the Lord are like Mount Zion, which cannot be shaken but endures forever. As the mountains surround Jerusalem, so the Lord surrounds his people both now and forevermore." As Susan reflected on the verse, she knew that the Lord was telling her that He surrounded Ireland.

On that same morning, Kelly took some time to pray. He felt inspired to write in his journal the words that he felt the Holy Spirit was speaking to him:

Kenmare, Ireland. 8:24 AM. *This is the land of your forefathers who neither knew God nor served Him... They were not nobles of the land but are the people of the land. They fell short, for the Word was not with them. I, the Lord God, will lift the veil over this land because of the prayers of a few for the Light to shine on this land. The Light will shine in the not so distant future and many have I chosen as bearers of the Light. Do not be afraid, do not fear the mission, but seek it with all your heart. My spirit will be poured out to bring life to this land. My blood has been shed and it will purify and wash anew. My servants I will send and my words will be given to them.*
Your call is here. I will open the doors. Speak with those you encounter and see if my Word, the true Word, doesn't find the heart...

My gospel will not be found short or given in complicated words, but in the truth of its simplicity.

Later that day, as they talked to locals, they discovered some interesting information. Since the 1990s, Ireland had fallen into a major crisis of faith. For various reasons, the young Irish were losing their trust in religious institutions. It seemed that the faith of an entire generation had been shipwrecked on the shore of doubt and disillusionment. Yet, it was clear that the Lord continued to surround the Irish and wanted to draw them back to His heart. Both Kelly and Susan were astonished at how clearly God spoke to each of them.

As the family enjoyed the remainder of their European holiday, Kelly and Susan continued to wonder: Is it really possible for God to uproot our lives and move us to Ireland? It was hard to believe that a particular verse, Deuteronomy 11:7-12, was how this whole thing started. Maybe once they returned to the States, the Irish-mania would fade away and both Kelly and Susan would realize this was all just a misunderstanding.

The day after they returned home from vacation, Leah, their 5-year-old daughter, asked Susan for a photo of the sheep of Ireland. Because she could not yet read, she had a small photo album of pictures as prayer reminders. Curious, Susan asked why she wanted the photo. She felt the air leave her lungs when Leah replied, "I want to pray for the people of Ireland." Out of the mouth of her daughter, God reminded Susan of His will for the family.

Over the next few weeks, the Currys searched for Christian ministries that worked in Ireland in hopes they could partner with an experienced organization to send them out. But none could be found. Slightly discouraged, they both felt it was essential that the Lord should guide their next step.

Dr. Bruce Wilkinson was scheduled to speak at a retreat at the end of July, which the Currys planned to attend. Kelly and Susan decided it was time to share with Bruce, a man who was instrumental in Kelly's faith journey and who could provide them with solid biblical counsel. Bruce was currently raising volunteers and funds for a multi-denominational movement sending Christian workers and teachers to Russia, which had just opened up to the West. He spent a good portion of the retreat talking about following the call of God in obedience, regardless of the cost. A video was shown of people who had actually made radical decisions to go to Russia with this CoMission, before the door of evangelism possibly closed again. Kelly and Susan cried while watching the video. Faced with the testimonies of these men and women who had moved to Russia out of radical obedience, the same kind of radical obedience the Currys were wrestling with putting into practice, they recognized it as yet another confirmation of their own call.

Later that evening, Bruce took time to talk with the Currys. He listened to Kelly's story about the call he had received from the Lord. Sharing the scripture from Deuteronomy that God had given him, Kelly told Bruce about the little signs that popped up everywhere they went, about their recent trip to Ireland, and all the ways that it seemed like God was speaking to him. When Kelly finished, Bruce stayed quiet for a moment. Then he slowly turned to Susan.

Looking her in the eyes he asked, "Susan, are you called to Ireland?"

In that moment, Susan knew that the weight of providence was in the next words she spoke. She felt as if the Lord, not Bruce, looked into her eyes. The Holy Spirit, not Bruce, asked the question. God gave her a choice. Kelly sat motionless, not knowing how she would answer, as up to now, he had not heard about her own vision of the cottage.

"Yes," she whispered.

At that point Susan finally shared with Kelly and Bruce the image she had recorded in her journal nearly a year before. Both Susan's vision of the cottage and the word of God testified to the call to Ireland. But it was that unadorned "yes" that changed the direction of their lives. That three-letter affirmation of God's will opened the door to Ireland. There was no turning back.

They took a few more minutes to discuss the logistics of a ministry overseas. As they talked, the Currys knew there was a foundational step that had to be taken to move forward on the journey. Kelly and Susan needed a proper Biblical education before they started toward Ireland.

⁓

Ravencrest Bible School, in Estes Park, Colorado, had a one-year intensive program where the students surveyed the entirety of the Old and New Testament. In addition, they offered courses on practical ministry. Kelly had been researching the school. When he asked Bruce if it would be a good idea for them to attend, Bruce replied, "Absolutely! When are you going?" Almost without thinking, Kelly said, "Tomorrow I am going back to work and resigning."

Drawn closer than ever by Susan's acknowledgment of their mutual call, Kelly and Susan stayed up most of that night, sitting on their bed, praying and planning. What sort of adventure had they gotten themselves into?

But by the time they were on the return flight home from the retreat, Susan was mentally listing a hundred reasons why the move was impossible. Natalie and Leah were still young. What would this mean for them? There was sectarian violence going on in Ireland. How could they bring their children into that? What about all the stuff they owned? Do they sell it, give it away, or put it in storage? And moving to Colorado for a year? They were used to sunny Florida.

Colorado had snow; lots and lots of snow. What about finances? What about leaving friends and family? How would they handle the loneliness?

The "what-ifs" filled Susan's mind. Weighing the issues, Susan began to bargain with God that maybe they should wait until their girls grew up. Then they would obey. Then they would go anywhere. She opened her Bible to where she had left off the day before. Now in Proverbs 3, she read verse 28, "Do not say to your neighbor, 'Come back tomorrow and I'll give it to you'— when you now have it with you." With tears streaming, she knew that the time was now. Susan knew she could not turn away from her promise to God.

The next morning, Kelly went to work to put in his notice. Before Kelly could walk into his office, his boss came to him. "Kelly, I have something I want to talk to you about."

His boss began to explain that he planned some exciting changes that would double the size of the company within three years. This growth time would provide great opportunities for Kelly. This was the chance of a lifetime. Only a few months before, this prospect would have been music to Kelly's ears. Kelly weighed his next words carefully.

"You know there have been a lot of changes in my life recently. In the past, the Lord called me to do a work for Him but I said no. I am not going to do that anymore. I was actually coming to you this morning to resign. I'm going to Bible College in preparation to go to Ireland." His boss stood stunned at Kelly's confession and decision. "I'll stay as long as I need to in order to transition my work, but this is something I feel compelled to do." Though surprised, Kelly's boss supported Kelly's decision. That same day, the couple enrolled for the January 1995 semester at Ravencrest Bible School.

Kelly had a new lease on life. Over the fall, he helped create a smooth transition for his successor, and they started the process of simplifying their household to prepare for the big move. It was toward the end of the year, as he cleaned out his garage, that the enormity of his choices and the upcoming changes hit him. His career was over. They were paring down most of the stuff they had collected over the years. And his kids' lives were about to be turned upside down. But when Kelly turned away from his job and the opportunities being offered, he had voluntarily walked away from his greatest temptation—more power. Now Kelly felt totally free to do whatever the Lord might ask.

Meanwhile, Susan struggled with leaving the close relationships in her life. The challenge of letting go of the people around her even made it hard to leave behind items that were symbolic of her relationships. None of her possessions signified personal relationships more than her pictures. Yet God was asking Susan to grab hold of Him instead of finding her security in human connections. One morning, little Leah came to Susan, still rubbing the sleep from her eyes. "Mommy, I had a weird dream."

"What did you dream?" asked Susan.

A worried look came over Leah's face. "I dreamed the house was on fire and you were getting us out of the house." Susan became very interested. "Daddy pulled us out and I grabbed my dolls. Then Daddy took us over to the neighbors, but you kept running back into the house and getting things."

By now, Susan sensed this was no ordinary dream. "Leah, what was I running back to get?" she asked with curiosity.

"Pictures, Mommy. You were grabbing all of the pictures of everyone." Once again, out of the mouth of her child, God spoke to Susan. She knew it was time to lay aside anything that hindered the move. Packing her photos away, Susan knew they represented the sentiment of home and that she was clinging to the mementos of her relationships for stability. She kept the photos, but now clung to God as her stability. There was no stronger steadiness than in the One who was now leading her family into His will.

Kelly, on the other hand, had a different collection to let go of. Over the last few years, he had collected nine classic Corvettes. But by this time, as he continued to surrender power over his life to God, Kelly had lost any sense of attachment to the Corvettes. He could not take them to Colorado or Ireland. And he certainly could not take them to Heaven. So one by one, he sold them to reinvest the value of each car into something of eternal value.

In order to brave the snow of Colorado, they purchased a cherry-red, four-wheel drive Suburban, an almost impossible find at that time in Florida. This was yet another answer to myriad prayers over the details of their move. In mid-December, Kelly, Susan, Natalie and Leah packed up all their necessary belongings into the back of the truck. They headed to Kentucky to spend Christmas with family and then hit the highway for Colorado.

The road to Ireland began in the Rockies.

Chapter 6

Walking on the Waves

The One who calls you is faithful and He will do it.
1 Thessalonians 5:24 (NIV)

*With your help I can advance against a troop;
with my God I can scale a wall.*
Psalm 18:29 (NIV)

WHEN THE RED SUBURBAN PULLED INTO Estes Park, Colorado, on December 31, 1994, the winds were gusting at a temperature well below zero. The Floridians had driven into a crystal-white mountainous wonderland. They did not mind the temperature outside until they entered their new home. The heating was not working. While the family shivered, Kelly stoked the fire. They all slept on the floor in front of the fireplace that first night, thawing out around the blazing fire. Despite the cold, Kelly and Susan were excited about where the Lord had led them.

The Currys had entered into a season of transition, just like those of other obedient followers written about in the Bible. How did Moses, a shepherd for forty years, become the man who would lead Israel out of Egyptian captivity? It would take a call, a decision, and time. What about the humble fishermen of Capernaum, casting nets to make ends meet and admiring Jesus from afar? What did their next few weeks look like after Jesus said to them, "Drop your nets and follow me?" Or how about Saul who was knocked to the ground on a nondescript road by the sudden presence of Jesus and stood up as Paul? He went to the desert for two years! For every call of God accepted by His people, there is a season of training, learning and adapting. The Currys did not simply drop everything and head to Ireland. It took months to discern the call of God, months to prepare for the transition, and now they would take many more months to learn the lessons that would equip them for the work ahead.

Bible school started in early January. Most of the incoming students had graduated high school just months before coming to Ravencrest. The Currys enjoyed connecting with their young classmates and often met them at the local coffee shop or opened their home for gatherings. The sense of community and the ecumenical mixture at Ravencrest began to change how the Currys prioritized the various aspects of Christian ministry. Community had been the core of Christianity from the beginning. Community was essential to the faith. Community was life. Wherever God was calling them, they knew that a community setting was going to be a part of it.

That year of Biblical studies was a joy for both Susan and Kelly. Besides a deepening love of the Scripture, the Ravencrest staff taught the Currys that discipline, good stewardship, and creative thinking are vital components to a healthy organization. Gentle grace and loving discipline must be traveling partners with the direction of God's spirit. Nourishing leadership recognizes that everyone is at a different place in their spiritual journey. Each leadership challenge must be considered carefully, prayerfully and clearly. Above all else, a healthy community of believers is one of the greatest undertakings of effective Christian leadership.

For the first time in his life, Kelly's world was in balance. This season of little lessons helped to build a large foundation of holistic, healthy ministry. The year at Ravencrest was one of the best years for the Currys. A restoration beyond their hopes took place in their marriage, family, and ministry.

～

In January of 1996, after graduating from Ravencrest, Kelly and Susan packed up the red Suburban for a second time and headed back to Kentucky. Over the next few months, they would continue to share their growing vision for Ireland with family and friends, asking for prayers for the unknown endeavor that lay ahead an ocean away.

While in school they had submitted several applications to mission organizations but they could only find one that even had the beginnings of operations in Ireland. Although they hoped to be sent through an already established organization, their leads proved unfruitful. As much as they wanted to avoid admitting this reality, it appeared the Lord was sending them to Ireland independently.

One day, while Kelly was out running errands, he came across *The Catechism of the Catholic Church* in the bookstore. When he saw the massive book he heard the Holy Spirit whisper to him, "*Kelly, you need to buy this.*"

Kelly was an avid reader. He already had stacks of books in his 'to read' pile. He thought, "Why do I need to add another huge book to my must-reads?" He started to walk away but that familiar voice whispered again.

"*Kelly, I want you to read this. Are you going to do this your way or My way?*"

He bought the book and moved it to the top of his reading list. As Kelly read through the Catechism, he found it illuminating. He jotted down a list of questions about the Catholic faith and decided to go see a priest from the local Catholic Church in Owensboro, Kentucky, where he had attended as a child. He explained he wanted to better understand the Catholic teaching as the Lord was sending him to Ireland. Kelly was already getting a sense that the Lord was encouraging him to see the commonalities of the Christian denominations rather than focus on what divided them.

"I have been reading the Catechism and I have a few questions."

The priest was surprised at Kelly's request, but agreed to meet with him. Their connection was immediate. A friendship developed as they visited several times over the next three months to discuss the Bible and the specifics of the Catholic faith. This was, once again, a season of unexpected training, arranged by the Holy Spirit to prepare the Currys for the foreign land He was leading them to. Zeal and passion alone would not be enough for a lasting and fruitful ministry. They required thorough and focused training.

~

Throughout the year at Ravencrest, the Currys had prayed over a map of Ireland that they had hung on the refrigerator, asking God where they were to go when they arrived. During family times, they read though an old travel book, learning as much as possible about the different towns and counties, yet no specific direction came to mind.

In May of that year, Kelly purchased the family's airplane tickets to Shannon, Ireland's western port of entry. He chose to fly into this airport solely on the basis that they had flown through it previously on their vacation to Ireland two years before. They booked three weeks' worth of accommodations in different locations, thinking they would just arrive and see where the Lord led them.

Kelly and Susan often discussed where they were going to plant their ministry. As they prayed over a map and read the travel books a particular city had come to both of their minds but they were afraid to share their thoughts, each uncertain as to whether they had heard God's voice since they had not even visited it on their trip. They were both surprised to hear that each felt that they had a leading to a specific place. Neither Kelly nor Susan wanted to say the name first because they were afraid of influencing the other. They finally agreed to say the name of the city at the same time. The anticipation was palpable.

"1...2...3... GALWAY."

The same city came out of both their mouths.. They had read about the seaside town in their travel books, but hadn't really discussed it as an option. They had no particular reason why they both felt led to move to there. The only thing they now agreed on was that Galway was where God was leading them. Somehow He had quickened their hearts to this location. Months of prayer and wondering ended with GALWAY.

But that did not answer the constant question people were asking the Currys. "What are you going to do when you get to Ireland?" "The only thing we know is that we are not supposed to plant a church," was Kelly and Susan's only response. "God will lead us where He wants us to be and show us what He wants us to do."

The reaction from many of those querying about their actions was a look that said, 'Are you stupid or just crazy?' At times, Kelly and Susan encountered negative attitudes from Christians who could not equate their personal view of God's will with what was happening in the Currys' lives. But the couple continued to grow in confidence that the Lord was in control. When the time was right, the Holy Spirit would guide them along the path.

They had become accustomed to probing questions. These were welcomed because the questions of others they respected could help them hone the vision as the Lord directed. Godly wisdom could save them from pitfalls they might normally overlook. However, sometimes the questions caused discouragement. A well-meaning Christian acquaintance once asked, "Why would God send you to Ireland? You could accomplish a lot more by staying in your job and sending money." Somewhat disheartened, Kelly and Susan asked themselves an important question: Does God want us to give money to works in Ireland instead of going over there and establishing a ministry? It was Dr. Bruce Wilkinson's counsel that strengthened them in their questioning.

"God owns the cattle on a thousand hills. He doesn't need your money. God needs your obedience." That settled their minds completely. They put down a spiritual marker on the road and moved on; God was faithful to confirm and reconfirm so many times.

Details still needed to be sorted. Now that they had decided on Galway, they had to figure out what to do with the three weeks of reservations that they could not cancel. There was also the task of how to move their belongings with only a small rental car.

A friend from Ravencrest contacted the Currys, knowing that their move to Ireland was imminent. He knew someone else who was moving to Ireland and thought they might want to contact him. Jim's parents were both from Ireland but he had been born and raised in the U.S. Now he and his family were moving over shortly ahead of the Currys. As they talked by phone, Jim offered their home as a place to stay when the Currys' temporary accommodations ended. "Where's your home located?" asked Kelly. The response came, "Galway. Will that work?" They even offered to pick up the Currys' extra luggage at the airport until the Currys could arrive in Galway three weeks later. Kelly smiled at the Lord's provision. God already had the details covered.

When the moment arrived for the Currys to leave the U.S. for Ireland, they were ready. Their transition from their old life to a new call was complete. It was time to obey Christ and walk on the waves.

～

In early August, the Currys arrived in Ireland with six boxes of books and eleven suitcases. Their plan was simple. While their baggage preceded them to Galway, they would get acquainted with Ireland by spending two weeks in County Cork and then a week in County Sligo, where Kelly had been told his ancestors had lived 150 years before. They took this time to pray for God's direction. During that first month, a sense of peace steadied their steps and their hearts.

After a few days of rest, they headed into Cork, the second largest city in Ireland, to shop for a car. The day they arrived, Oasis, one of the UK's most popular rock bands at that time, was holding a concert in the city. The streets were packed with young people waiting for the concert venue to open. Coming from Florida, a prime retirement area of the U.S., to a country where 50% of the population was under 30 years old was eye opening to Kelly and Susan. The streets buzzed with activity.

The overwhelming images of tens of thousands of young people in the lanes and boulevards of Cork led the Currys to enquire about the state of Ireland's youth. Was there any Christian influence on the young people? Nobody seemed to know. If 50% of the population was so young, then who was reaching them with the message of Christ? That day, something began to stir in Kelly and Susan.

The next morning, over a cup of tea, the Currys discussed a flood of ideas for their future Galway ministry. During their individual time with the Lord that morning, each of them was given a different piece to the puzzle. When they came back together, they began to put together the clear directives the Lord was speaking to them. A picture of an Irish ministry was beginning to form.

They were to build a community haven for young people, a safe place for them to hang out. It would provide a coffee house atmosphere where conversation could flow easily over a hot cup of tea and a scone along with a bookshop that offered quality reading and good music for those seeking a deeper faith walk.

Looking at the newspaper the next morning, they saw a huge picture on the front page of the Cork Independent. Thousands of young people stood, hands upraised, for the members of Oasis as they played for the masses. "What's the alternative?" Kelly wondered aloud. The photo was another confirmation that they had finally heard solid direction from the Lord. With a clearer vision, Kelly and Susan were now ready to get to Galway.

While they stayed at Jim's home, they began to look for a permanent residence. Their prayers were specific about the amenities they hoped for in their home, such as furnishings, bookshelves, and windows to bring in more light on the dark and rainy days. In two weeks, God provided a home almost identical to what they had been praying for, right down to a farmhouse stove in the kitchen.

As they settled into their new Irish home, Kelly and Susan knew there was no turning back. Everything had been theory up to this point. Now they would learn by experience. Even more important, they were confident in God's leading.

～

When John F. Kennedy was trying to convince Americans that sending a man to the moon, a seemingly impossible feat, was possible, he told this story.

Like most Irish boys in the late 1800s, Patrick Joseph Kennedy, (JFK's grandfather) merely endured school. The real adventures began on his way home from the classroom. If the day was bright, PJ and the lads would cut across the lush farm fields as a shortcut home. A little bit of exploration was a chance to delay the daily farm work that always hung over their thatched-roofed homes, like an approaching afternoon rain.

One afternoon, PJ and his friends decided to inspect the seemingly unscalable walls of the huge spectral estate that sat on the edge of their village. For half an hour they walked along the barrier, feeling the granite-flecked rock under their fingertips. The boys knew that there had to be a place to climb over. Generations of penniless village boys and girls had wondered what treasure or danger was behind the soaring stone walls.

PJ's fervent curiosity often drove him to investigate where others ignored. He imagined aloud about how he might climb the wall for a peek at the mysterious estate grounds. The only visible way through the wall was a well-guarded gate. He had to find another way over. But his optimistic talk caused the lads to jeer.

"Hey, boyo - it would take a ladder the size of an oak tree to make it to the other side. We've looked everywhere. There's no way over. It's hopeless, PJ. You'll never make it."

PJ looked at his friends, then furrowed his brow as he thought through a grand plan in his mind. He deliberately turned and looked from the dirt on the ground next to the wall to the stones on the top of the wall, calculating some secret formula that might change the reality of the situation. Then PJ did something that caused bugged eyes and a collective gasp from all the boys.

PJ took his expensive hat and tossed it over the wall.

His father had given him the hat for his fourteenth birthday. It was PJ's pride and joy. All his friends knew the handsome hat came with a promise from his father: "Lad, your mother and I saved for a year to buy you this hat. You best not come home if you lose it, because you'll receive the beating of your life. Happy birthday, son."

The gang hushed and looked at PJ like he had lost his mind. With the confidence of a seasoned explorer, PJ smiled as he looked into the stunned eyes of each boy before he said, "Now I have to find a way over."

And he did.

There are many in our world determined to climb walls thought to be unscalable. They 'toss the hat' and find a way over. The Currys had tossed their hat into the city of Galway.

Now that the family had a place to grow roots, it was time to find the way for the ministry vision to come to life. Unlike the Currys finding a home, the next step was not so easy.

Chapter 7

Foundations

By the grace God has given me, I laid a foundation as a wise builder, and someone else is building on it. But each one should build with care. For no one can lay any foundation other than the one already laid, which is Jesus Christ.
1 Corinthians 3:10-11 (NIV)

Have I not commanded you? Be strong and courageous. Do not be afraid; do not be discouraged, for the Lord your God will be with you wherever you go.
Joshua 1:9 (NIV)

BEFORE MOVING TO IRELAND, THE CURRYS formed a stateside charity called Foundation in Christ Ministries to help fund their work in Ireland. The name of the non-profit organization, suggested by their young daughter Natalie, was a declaration of what the Currys had come to believe in the depth of their beings: "By the grace God has given me, I laid a foundation as a wise builder, and someone else is building on it. But each one should build with care. For no one can lay any foundation other than the one already laid, which is Jesus Christ." (1 Corinthians 3:10-11).

The foundation they would build upon in Ireland was laid over seventeen hundred years ago by saints and scholars who invested their lives in the proclamation of Christ's message among the wild Celts of Éire. The same Jesus who sought after the heart of the elementary school atheist and a woman who, in her grief and sorrow, abandoned God was the same Jesus who was the cornerstone of Ireland. That same Jesus still had a call on the Irish.

Throughout the rest of 1996, Susan settled the family into their home while Kelly began to introduce himself to the Christian leadership in Galway. For the first few weeks he sought out local ministers: Catholic priests, Anglican vicars, Presbyterian ministers, non-denominational pastors. Not a handshake was missed. Kelly wanted to understand the atmosphere of the Christian community in Ireland.

Much of what he discovered disheartened him. Age-old hurts, stemming from the British occupation of the country that had outlawed Catholicism in favor of Anglicanism, were still obvious in the modern-day churches. The Catholics did not trust the non-Catholics, and the non-Catholics disliked anything that even appeared to be Roman Catholic. Anglicans, once a political powerhouse, were now a minority. The non-Catholic churches were typically small congregations. The traditional denominations, non-denominational churches, Evangelicals, and Pentecostals were struggling to add members. To Kelly and Susan, the odds of working cross-denominationally, as they felt called to do, appeared overwhelming because most of the Christians believed it would take too much compromise. It seemed as if the only thing many of these brothers and sisters in Christ had in common was a mutual distrust for each other.

As Kelly began to pour out his heart for Ireland, some ministers shrugged off the Currys' mission, probably believing that Kelly and Susan, like many other "missionaries" before them, would become discouraged and eventually leave. In a city where Christian ministry was difficult already, another group might only cloud the waters.

One pastor of a small church even said, "Thanks for coming, but you are not needed here. We have it covered."

The following morning, Susan was so troubled that she said to Kelly, "If nobody wants us, why did we come? Why don't we just go home?"

The move had been hard. They were all missing family and friends, the girls were struggling to adjust, and the future didn't look promising. Kelly tried to encourage Susan, but nothing he said broke through her despair. Finally he said, "You'll have to get your answer from God."

Her answer came in prayer. She sensed the Lord asking her, "Did the pastor ask you to come?"

"No." was her reply.

"Did the Irish ask you to come?"

Again she replied, "No."

"Then who was it that asked you to come?" came the Lord's final word.

Susan knew that this call was God's design, not hers, not Kelly's, and certainly not that of any church or individual in Galway. Kelly and Susan had no fantastic plan to lead souls to Christ. In fact, they barely knew what they were doing. But they were there for a purpose that would be revealed in God's time.

In spite of the discouragement they received from some people, Kelly and Susan were warmly welcomed by others, and graciously received among the Catholics in their neighborhood. Kelly began to attend a local prayer group where a kindly party of Catholic laypeople, led by a priest, read Scripture and reflected on what God was saying to them and the Church through the Word of God. They were using an ancient practice of Bible study called Lectio Divina. On a couple of occasions, the priest even asked Kelly to lead the study.

Breda McDonough, a Catholic lay leader in Galway, remembered those studies. "I was completely fascinated with this joy-filled Baptist minister with the southern drawl. His accent was strange to our ears but his faith was inspirational. We'd never witnessed a non-Catholic so on fire for Christ. He had a faith founded on God's Holy Scripture."

The friendliness, acceptance and hunger for God's Word that Kelly witnessed among the Catholic community were contradictory to the views of Catholicism expressed by many of the non-Catholics he had talked with on both sides of the Atlantic. Ireland was a religiously and politically complicated place, and Kelly and Susan had much to learn.

By early 1997, the Curry family had started to acclimate to Irish culture. They established a sister charity in Ireland for Foundation in Christ Ministries and felt the Lord's prompting to initiate the ministry. It was time to purchase a piece of property, an incredibly difficult undertaking under Ireland's vibrant economy at the time.

In the early 1990s, Ireland was one of the poorest countries in Europe. Considered a backwater nation by many Europeans, she then went through a colossal economic transformation. A number of factors, including an Irish cultural boom triggered by worldwide acclaim for artists like Riverdance and U2, membership into the European Union, an unprecedented surge in tourism, and a state-driven economic development program, coincided to produce powerful results for the Irish economy. By the late 1990s, Ireland had become one of the wealthiest countries in Europe.

In less than ten years, Ireland had moved from an agricultural economy into a technological one. Many families that had lived hand to mouth for as long as they could remember now had the disposable cash to buy material goods. Unfortunately, the financial growth also had a devastating effect on church attendance. As materialism increased, the desire for a spiritual life decreased. Labeled by economists as the Celtic Tiger, the exploding economy also produced a property-buying mania.

For months, Kelly and Susan phoned several real estate offices. They walked throughout Galway looking for a piece of property near the heart of the city that might work as a base of operations for the ministry. Whenever they inquired about a for-sale sign on a building, they were told the property was already sold. Suitable rental property was equally hard to find. This happened countless times—they would see a building, phone the auctioneer, only to learn that the building was already sold or leased. Then they walked away discouraged as they waited for the next opportunity.

By early spring of that year, the Currys wondered if there was any property left in Galway. All they could do was look and wait for God to open the right door, at the right price, and in the right location.

―

Kelly and Susan did not want the focal point of their time in Ireland to be solely spent looking for property. They began to pray for God to use them in a more significant way, whether they had a building or not.

Since Easter was coming up, they focused on a different project. It was time to make a bold proclamation. Kelly and Susan both loved Campus Crusade's *Jesus Film*, a presentation of the Gospel of Luke that has been shown around the world to millions of people in their native tongue. Taking out ads in the local newspapers, they decided to show the movie at the beginning of the Lenten season. After obtaining the film, the equipment and a movie screen, they rented large meeting rooms in two hotels for two consecutive nights. It was a gamble. Would anyone show up? Would the four Currys be the only ones watching the film?

Before advertising the event, they settled on a couple of important factors. Unlike past practices, there would be no altar calls. They strongly believed that they were not called to convert people from one Christian denomination to another, but to encourage a deep and growing faith in Christ. Also, at the end of the presentation they would offer a six-week study over the Gospel of John.

A few local pastors were disappointed when Kelly would not allow them to pass out their church flyers during the showing. Kelly had become convinced that in a city of two hundred Protestants and thousands of Catholics, he was to handle the night in a low-key way.

Since all of the dialogue in the movie was taken directly from Luke's Gospel, the Bible would speak the truth. The prayer at the end of the movie was directly from Scripture and Kelly trusted that the Holy Spirit would complete the work. Some non-Catholic church leaders at that time did not understand his unconventional approach, but Kelly felt certain this was the Lord's guidance for him.

To their delight, a total of 160 people attended over two evenings. When the film ended, the audience was silent, in awe of the story of Christ. Kelly simply thanked the audience for coming and invited them to the Bible study.

Breda McDonough would later say about the evening, "They did it just right. Historically, every time a missionary came to Galway, they demanded we leave the (Catholic) church. Kelly and Susan did not ask us to leave our church. They asked us to embrace Christ."

Another attendee that night was Gerardine Weir. "I immediately knew there was something different with these two. So many people pay lip service with their faith, but in the Currys, I saw God, especially as they reached out to the fringes of society, to the people no one believed in. I witnessed, firsthand, their kindness and generosity time and time again." Gerardine had an answer for those who were suspicious of the Currys' intentions. "I told them that I've seen more of God reflected in the Currys than in most organizations."

For Easter, the Currys ran an ad in the Galway newspaper that celebrated the Resurrection of Christ. The ad proclaimed:

HE HAS RISEN!
CELEBRATE THIS EARTH SHATTERING EVENT
AT THE CHURCH OF YOUR CHOICE.

They realized the ad might draw a line in the sand between them and some of the local Christians. They certainly did not want to offend any fellow believer, but they trusted the Lord's leading. Repeatedly, they remembered a phrase they had heard to "Keep the main thing the main thing." The Currys were in Galway to proclaim Jesus, not denominations or theologies or philosophies. Jesus had died to rescue all people out of sin and destruction, both non-believers and churchgoers. He longed to save all who called upon His name. Whatever a person's position in Christ—whether being introduced to Him for the first time, rekindling a relationship that had grown apathetic with Him, or continuing to grow in a vibrant one—Christ alone was the essential message that compelled the Currys to reach out.

~

The hunt for a building continued but the results remained the same. Kelly and Susan scoured Galway but real estate was a scarce commodity. The scant available properties were either too much money, too small, in a poor location or not a good fit. A number of ideal properties went up for lease on Lower Dominick Street, a road at the edge of the City Centre, home to the city's artists and residents who pursued edgier and more alternative lifestyles. But Kelly always missed the opportunities by a hair's breadth. By the end of the summer, Kelly joked with Susan, "I can tell you one thing. When we do get property, it certainly won't be on Dominick Street."

On a sunny September morning, Kelly was standing near an auctioneer office when he saw a poster go up in the window for a prime piece of property. He immediately called Susan and they arranged to meet the realtor. But Kelly warned, "You're never going to believe it, Suz. It's on Lower Dominick Street. Don't get your hopes up."

When they showed up, the building was anything but ideal. Its red and yellow exterior was a poor covering for a building known as one of the worst hostels in Galway. Declining businesses near the location made it even less appealing. But there were three secondary schools and a large university less than a ten minute walk from the front door.

The old building was initially built as an Army barracks during the English occupation. In the early 1900s, it became a base for the infamous Black and Tans, a constabulary force set up to discourage Irish independence. Once Ireland gained independence, it was converted into a police station. By the 1950's, the location was the headquarters for the Council Engineers who controlled the water levels of the canals that snake through the city. The building's final fall from glory came in the 1980s, as it was taken over as a youth hostel. It quickly disintegrated both in structure and reputation.

There is one descriptive word given by those who remembered the hostel—nasty. As the Currys entered the hostel, which was still open for business, they quickly deduced that it was a haven for drug use. There were even people lying around in chemical induced stupors, surrounded by walls covered with freehand psychedelic paintings. Apparently, anyone with a brush and a joint could decorate. All their doubts burst to the surface. Was renovation even possible or was the hostel a throwaway property ready for demolition? Besides a palpable darkness in the building, the asking price was too high.

Despite the outward appearance, the Currys believed they were to move on the property immediately. They put a deposit down and brought the Board of Directors of the ministry over to view the property and to gather their thoughts, concerns and questions.

The board members quietly walked through the derelict property. It might have once been architecturally sound, but temporary choppy walls had been thrown up, distorting the interior architecture and erasing anything of historical significance. The spiritual atmosphere of the place was oppressive. Yet, they all knew that this was the first freestanding building that had opened up. Could God redeem a neglected and dilapidated building the same way He redeemed the dilapidated lives of people?

After taking some time to pray, the Board unanimously agreed to buy the building. The purchase was an extreme act of obedience. Once the papers were signed, they took a sweeping look at their new headquarters. "What have we done? This place is a right mess" was the thought on everyone's mind. By January of 1998, the building was ready for a major renovation.

―

When Cormac Murphy entered the doors for the first time, he considered the structure a lost cause. Cormac was a respected builder in Galway. He was introduced to Kelly by an architect who believed that he was the only man for the job. Kelly unlocked the door to the now empty building and let Cormac make a silent assessment. The look on Cormac's face did not bring Kelly any confidence in the choice of property.

"That building gave off some very bad vibes. Quite frankly, I saw no hope." recalled Cormac. But that didn't deter him.

"First of all, Kelly and I got on well right away. He's a bit of a rascal and a sharp businessman. We immediately knew we could work together. But truly, I was delighted to have the work and the price was right. I don't mind a good challenge."

Cormac and Kelly both agreed that to do the renovation correctly, the whole building needed to be gutted down to its original walls, foundation to roof. As the building was emptied of all its faux walls, old furniture, ruined fixtures, and strange art, the darkness began to drain away like poison from a wound.

In the beginning, Cormac was a bit suspicious of the ministry. "I didn't know if they were a cult or if they'd try to convert me and my workers. But Kelly always encouraged me to go to my church. He is a man who lives his faith."

Many mornings, right before the workers arrived, Kelly and Susan would go to the building to pray over it, dedicating it to the

Lord's work. Cormac remembered the morning prayer meetings. "At first it was a strange sight. We'd arrive to see them worshiping like they were in church. We'd hear them pray for us. Something like that never happens on the work site."

The experience was an emotional one for Cormac. "Every time they prayed, the darkness lifted a bit more. They are genuine people and I saw a real faith through their actions." Others in the community began to come and pray over the building. "Every time someone came in and prayed, they left the building a little brighter," noted Cormac.

The challenges of renovation were intense and it took seven months to complete the process. Each predicament they encountered in the renovation was brought to the Lord in prayer. God's answers were surprising. Old molded plaster was removed to reveal the exceptional original stone walls. As they eliminated an ugly door at the front of the building, they discovered a stone-arched entry: a perfect portal for first impressions. An antique fireplace, enclosed by a false wall, was uncovered in the main sitting room. Stained carpeting and vinyl linoleum was removed to reveal beautiful old pitch pine floors, long unavailable since Ireland had been stripped of timber. Time after time, unique little architectural features were discovered during the renovation.

Cormac knew it was the prayers. "Things don't just happen in the building process. But no matter the challenges we faced, there was *always* an answer. I know it was the prayers."

~

It looked like Kelly and Susan's battles were coming to an end. Soon the building would be ready and the real work would begin. But an enemy they never imagined was starting to gain strength for a devastating sneak attack against Susan.

Family picture with Susan's mom on first "exploratory trip" to Ireland in 1994

Currys shortly after arriving in 1996 — Natalie, Kelly, Leah, Susan

The picture Susan took in 1994 of the thatch roofed cottages of Adare village

FICM Board visit to look at potential building before purchase—Pat Cregg, Dick Tatro, Dave Moreland, Shirley Moreland, Holly Johnson, Raymond Johnson, Natalie, Leah, & Kelly Curry

Renovations to the ground floor, hidden fireplace (L)

(Above) Hidden stone archway on ground floor
(L) Cormac Murphy on a tea break on the newly built stage

Part of the U.S. mission team, led by Bob Angelmeyer (in plaid shirt), in May 1998, tasked with painting the interior of the building

An Tobar Nua, newly renovated

Grand Opening Day: staff and some board members—Kelly, Natalie, Eamon Lynch, Susan, Leah, Holly Johnson, Raymond Johnson, Deborah Osburn, Pat Cregg

Moya Brennan performing on Grand Opening Day, August 1998

Grand Opening crowd waiting for Moya Brennan to perform

The first team and the Currys—Eamon Lynch, Julie Koehler, Natalie, Deborah Osburn, Leah, Susan and Kelly in August 1998

The galley- sized kitchen: (above) Mike and Kelly; (R) Eamon Lynch; (below) Megan & Leah

The Café (L) and canal room (above) after second renovation in 2006

Renovations on new facility next door to An Tobar Nua: Cormac Murphy preserving the aspects of the original plaster, floor joists, etc., for historical purposes in 2006

The new construction facing the canal with the original structure on the right

June and Dr. Arden Autry, first director of Emmaus Scripture School

Return visit of Kathy: (L to R) Tommy, Kathy Hegarty, Natalie, and Mike

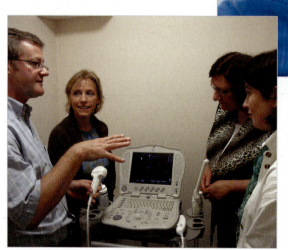

(Above) Tommy listening to a student in the Café

(L) Demonstration of the portable ultrasound machine for the crisis pregnancy ministry in 2006 (Susan second from left, Anne Buckley on right)

Megan, Leah and Natalie Curry

An Tobar Nua team in Spring 2014, finishing a lunch rush in the crazy little kitchen

Annual staff retreat in 2011

Keeping up with the lunch rush demand for hot chocolates - Kevin McNena

A friendly face in the bookstore - Deirde Morris

The ever expanding team of An Tobar Nua in 2014

An Tobar Nua in 2017

An evangelism training seminar being held in the Emmaus Scripture School classroom

A typical "Lunch Bunch" of students

The Famous Hot Dog hat

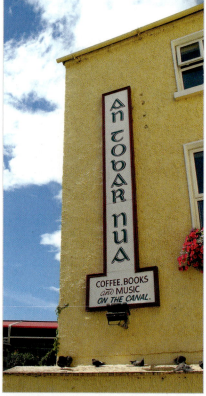

Mystery Theatre afternoon party with staff and students in 2017

Mike Shortt leading a student retreat in a school

Andrew Feeney leading worship for a large retreat group in a school

Kelly & Susan Curry

Tommy & Megan

2017 leadership: (L to R) John Shelton, Mike Shortt, Deirdre Morris, Andrew Feeney, Jimmy Earle

Spring 2017—An Tobar Nua team sharing breakfast after morning devotions

Chapter 8

An Tobar Nua

Everyone who drinks of this water will be thirsty again, but whoever drinks of the water that I will give him will never be thirsty again. The water that I will give him will become in him a spring of water welling up to eternal life.
John 4: 13-14 (ESV)

*Your people will volunteer freely
in the day of Your power.*
Psalm 110: 3 (NASB)

THE MAGNITUDE AND CONSISTENCY OF GOD'S faithful provision and leading hand in those early months in Ireland left the Currys in awe. An Tobar Nua, their base of operations in a bustling corner of Galway, is an example of God's goodness.

The large, historic building sits on a gently flowing canal. As you enter the building you will notice a seamless fusion of historical appreciation and modern architecture. This is one of the coolest communal establishments in the city and is now a well-known hangout for students of every age. Start wandering the building beyond the rambling rooms of the café and you will discover state of the art classrooms, counseling offices, comfortable housing for staff, and a quaint chapel that resonates with a saintly aura. An Tobar Nua has become the ecumenical heart for the Christian community in Galway.

Most people might be tempted to think that this grand achievement was created through some sort of brilliant master plan. People often ask questions like "Where did the resources come from? How did Kelly and Susan find such a great building on this ideal piece of property? How have they created an environment where Christians of every cut of the cloth work in harmony?" Some have said, "You have been really fortunate. How did you put all this together?"

But what most people do not realize is that everything they see —the beautiful windows, the stone arched doorway, the hot cups of tea, the smiling faces of the staff, and even the OPEN sign on the door - all of these 'accomplishments' came with a hard-fought battle. As the Currys know well, there is no neutral ground in the universe; every square inch, every split second is claimed by God or counterclaimed by the Enemy. An Tobar Nua has always been a spiritual battleground.

~

As Cormac's crew diligently toiled to restore the building, Kelly and Susan began the process of forming a ministry team. God had granted them an optimal location to open a small café that catered to the people of Galway, but especially to students. A café would be the ideal setting to establish a safe place for young people, but Kelly and Susan knew nothing about the restaurant business. There would be a significant learning curve to overcome. Their first task was to hire a cook. Kelly started asking some of the locals, and a pastor friend told Kelly he knew the man for the job.

Eamon Lynch is a hulking man who looks more like a Gaelic football player than a chef. Raised in the seaside town of Dundalk, near the border of Northern Ireland, Eamon learned to cook while serving in the Irish Army. While the Currys were building their team, Eamon was independently looking for a reason to move from his hometown. Every few weeks, Eamon visited friends in Galway, exploring any avenues that might bring him to the west of Ireland. As a committed Christ follower, Eamon desired to find a fulltime position in ministry, a near impossible feat in a country where most non-Catholic pastors were volunteers.

During one of his visits, Eamon was introduced to Kelly and Susan. Kelly said, "I immediately sensed Eamon was a gentle giant. Here was a young man who sincerely wanted to do God's will and who was also excited about cooking." But the job was still months away, so

Eamon did not put much weight in the possibility.

In the spring of 1998, Kelly called Eamon to ask him to come back to Galway for a formal interview. The conversation went extremely well and Eamon knew that a rare door was opening for him. Was it possible that he could be paid while serving Christ fulltime? Kelly hired him on the spot. Eamon became the ministry's first Irish employee.

Kelly decided to show Eamon the building on Lower Dominick Street where the ministry would be based. Eamon shared his first impressions of the yellow and red ex-hostel: "Man, it was rough; a real dump. But I knew by Kelly's full-on personality that this place was going to change. For some reason, I knew this would be a beautiful building when they were done."

In June of that year, Eamon moved to Galway with only £86 in his pocket. He would spend the next few weeks helping to put the finishing touches on the building.

Several other key people had to be put in place before the grand opening in August. Kelly and Susan knew that they needed volunteers to staff the café. Not only would the volunteer staff have to learn to cook and serve food, but they also needed to feel a call to reach students with the love of Christ. That meant an aptitude to listen, the capacity to pray with people and the ability to have fun. That summer, the Lord faithfully provided two young women from America, Julie Koehler and Deborah Osburn, who raised their own support to serve at the café for a year.

The main draw of the café would be serving lunches to students, due to the fact that none of the surrounding schools had cafeterias or provided lunch. Students either brought something from home to eat or bought food at local fast-food "chippers" or newsagents to eat on nearby benches or while dodging raindrops on their way back to school. Students were not generally welcomed by local restaurants and cafes, as they stayed long, bought little and pushed out potential adult customers. Uniquely, the café would offer affordable lunches and a variety of desserts, in addition to ample indoor seating, which they hoped would give students, as well as adults, the incentive to stop in. The staff's mission to reach students was simple—learn their names, find out their needs, and be there for them if they wanted to talk to someone. The café needed to be a safe haven for students, giving them a positive location where they could spend their "off" time. In addition, Bible studies would be offered for anyone interested.

Everything was falling into place as the opening date drew near. The final (and biggest) decision was what to call the new café. The name needed to resound in the Irish heart and paint a clear picture of what the Lord wanted to do through the ministry. It could not be too religious and it had to tell a story.

Some Irish friends, Pat and Ger Cregg, often spoke of re-digging the spiritual wells of their forefathers just as Isaac had reopened the wells dug by his father Abraham in Genesis 26. They suggested the name An Tobar Nua, Gaelic for The New Well.

The name resonated with the Currys who were touched by the story in the Gospels of a Samaritan woman that Jesus met at a well. The woman had wandered through life looking for God in all the wrong places. Then the day came when God came looking for her. Jesus met her alone, at a well, and answered her deepest longing:

"Jesus said to her, 'Everyone who drinks of this water will be thirsty again, but whoever drinks of the water that I will give him will never be thirsty again. The water that I will give him will become in him a spring of water welling up to eternal life.'"

In Ireland, pubs were the modern-day equivalent to the wells of Jesus's day. They were the place where the community congregated and shared life over a pint of Guinness. There were even pubs called An Tobar, but none served a different sort of drink: living water.

They agreed. The name would be *An Tobar Nua*.

—

Moya Brennan, the lead singer of the popular Irish band Clannád, was going to be appearing in Galway for the release of her first Christian album on the weekend of the grand opening. The Creggs, who knew Moya, contacted her about performing on opening day. Unbelievably, she agreed to appear for free in support of the vision of An Tobar Nua. This was the final surprise. The café doors were ready to be opened.

On August 8, 1998, the doors opened with a grand celebration. Word had traveled fast through the streets of Galway. The café was packed within the first hour, reaching its full capacity. Half of the multitude had turned up to see Moya Brennan. The other half turned up to see who was really coming because they did not believe it would be such a big name artist. Free appetizers and drinks satisfied the swarm. People toured the building and they were amazed at the beauty of the reconstruction. The small Christian bookshop in the back of the building was a special draw for believers.

The crowds were delighted. Laughter and joy filled a structure that, just a few months earlier, was a haven of darkness and desperation. As An Tobar Nua was officially declared open for business and dedicated to the work of Christ that day, the staff threw open the windows. An overflow crowd filled the canal walkway outside of the building so they could enjoy the afternoon concert by Moya.

Opening day was a hit. Kelly and Susan stood hand in hand looking out over the crowd. They soaked up the smiling faces and lightness in the atmosphere. The breeze coming through the windows felt like the refreshing wind of God's Spirit. Both thought about all the battles and struggles they endured until this moment. Kelly turned to Susan and whispered in her ear. "Hey hon. Maybe this *will* work."

―

The grand opening had been a success and now the staff had a few weeks to get into a rhythm before the school year started. Their initial menu was sparse: basic sandwiches, soup, and chips (French fries). A few pastries were ordered from a bakery and American chocolate chip cookies were made on site. There were a lot of kinks to work out, including the kitchen being the size of a postage stamp. Three people had to somehow fit into a space no bigger than a ship galley.

Everyone hoped the previous crowd would return, but in the weeks following, hardly anyone entered the place. Ten people in eight hours accounted for a stellar day. The staff was eating more than they were selling. School was beginning and they wondered how they could encourage students to come to what looked like a dead business. In hindsight, the low crowds were a blessing. Those quiet days allowed the staff to become a team. They developed creativity and discussed what they might do to draw students through their doors. As they prayed together, they became a family. It was during those days that one of their secret weapons was unveiled: An Tobar Nua's American cookie jazzed up with icing.

In Ireland, the traditional tea cookie is called a biscuit and the softer cookies popular in America are given that label—American cookies. The chocolate chip cookie was a special favorite, and adding buttery icing between two cookies created a real hit. Anything American was a novelty and sold well. Soon, the café would become the place to get a tasty lunch. It would be another year before additions to the menu, such as hotdogs and burritos, came along, and eventually the café began to short order cook new foods and bake the café's own desserts. But even as the café took its first baby steps, Kelly and Susan were back in the fight. And this one would be for Susan's life.

―

In the last week of July, while the team was preparing for the opening of An Tobar Nua, Susan had discovered a small lump in her breast. With no family history of cancer, she did not have an immediate concern. Kelly and Susan casually shared what was happening with the ministry's Board members who had arrived for the grand opening, yet the Currys encouraged everyone to focus on the opening.

In late August, Susan went to a specialist who, after a needle-biopsy, said he was 95% certain the lump was benign. Even with a negative test, he explained that there was a 5% chance that something might have been missed. He strongly suggested that the lump be removed. Susan and Kelly sighed in relief and agreed to have the surgery.

The week before the minor surgery, one of their prayer partners in the U.S. emailed Susan that she had felt an urgency to pray for the family and asked if they were well. Susan replied "yes." A few days later the woman emailed Susan back. She could not shake the feeling that she needed to pray specifically for Susan. Only then did Susan think of her impending surgery. She shared the upcoming procedure with this prayer warrior but still felt no concern, even wondering, with the school year only beginning, if she should postpone the surgery for a while.

On September 6, three days before the operation, Susan was praying for the Lord to bring her into a deeper relationship with Him. She recorded the following in her journal: "I feel like a child on tiptoe, peering at something out of reach. Lord, grow me to Your next level." In His quiet way, the Lord spoke to Susan's heart that He had heard her and that she was to depend on Him. The following day, in the midst of her prayer, these words came to her: "*Susan, the enemy seeks to conquer, but I am your victory.*" Susan was puzzled. There were huge battles behind them. No doubt there would be new conflicts ahead, but right now things were moving forward. Still not connecting the Lord's words with the upcoming surgery, Susan felt assured of His promise.

Two days later, in a staggering blow, the surgery revealed that Susan had breast cancer. A second surgery would be required to check the surrounding area and lymph nodes.

Kelly felt shell-shocked as he held his crying wife. How could this have happened when everything was just starting to go right? For the next few days, through the distress and overwhelming diagnosis, the couple painfully made the prayerful decisions that were best for Susan's health and their family's future. But they felt a peace in moving forward with a temporary return to the U.S.

They sat down with the staff and shared the news. Kelly and Susan both saw fear and confusion in their eyes. Of course, the staff's first concern was Susan, but they also wondered what would happen to the ministry. Every one of them had moved to Galway and given up a year of their lives to serve Christ in this unique place. Would An Tobar Nua be shut down just a few weeks after opening? What about the students? Young people were finally showing up, asking questions, and opening up their lives.

Kelly shared with the staff that they would be going back to the States for Susan's second surgery and chemo treatments. Their family and friends were there to provide support and it would be the best place for their daughters, Natalie and Leah, while Susan recovered. They needed to take the battle for Susan's life day by day. It was time to trust the Lord. They assured the staff that the café was not Kelly and Susan's building, and ultimately it was not their ministry. An

Tobar Nua was God's vision and everyone sitting in that circle had come in obedience. Kelly asked the staff to take some time to think over what was happening and pray about their own next steps. They would come back as a team and decide what to do.

Leaving Ireland seemed unthinkable, especially when the café had only been open for a month. It was as though they had birthed a baby only to leave it behind. The grief was tangible. An Irish friend from church shared a story that brought comfort.

Their friend had been serving in a ministry in China but unfortunately, she had to leave China far sooner than she had planned. As she prayed for God to give her peace in her leaving and an opportunity to return to China, she found hope in the book of Exodus. Her ministry in China was like the baby Moses.

Moses' mother had placed Moses in the reed basket on the river to save his life from Pharaoh. Amazingly, Pharaoh's daughter found the floating baby Moses, saved the child, and brought in Moses' mother to raise him. Likewise, she had to place her ministry in the river of the Lord for His keeping.

Their friend held onto the hope that the Lord would allow her to return to China to help "raise her ministry," but first, she had to let it go to be raised by others. Letting go, in obedience to God, was the only thing that kept her ministry alive.

The meaning was clear to the Currys. The ministry was a newly-birthed babe and the Lord was asking them to release it back to Him. The ministry belonged to the Irish. He was gently removing it from their hands.

The next day, Eamon spoke to Kelly about the staff's decision, "We're going to stay. We'll do whatever it takes, as long as it takes, to keep An Tobar Nua runnin' until you return." Kelly and Susan were strengthened by his words. Their calling, spoken to them by God so many years ago, that burden of obedience to serve the youth of

Ireland, was no longer just theirs. Others were standing shoulder to shoulder with them, holding up their arms the way Aaron and Hur held up Moses' arms during Israel's battles. The small staff was a community of people banded together through their obedience to and love of Christ. An Tobar Nua was already becoming a well of healing.

Two weeks later, back in the U.S. for Susan's treatment, the Lord reminded them of the staff's courage, by pointing out Psalm 110:3, "Your troops will be willing on the day of your battle." (NIV) That verse became foundational for An Tobar Nua as they prayed over the years for God to reveal partners for the ministry.

It was during these moments of great struggle and potential disaster that the true meanings of sacrifice and love were defined for the ministry team. It was not in their victories or their abundance that they discovered their strength. Trial, tribulation, and weakness—it was in traversing those chasms that the Currys and the staff understood the reliability of the Holy Scripture and the Lord's steadfastness.

For the next several months, Eamon, with the support of the Creggs and the two American volunteers, kept An Tobar Nua afloat. Kelly came from the States once a month to keep up with the accounting and to encourage the team. Back in the U.S., all Susan could do was pray and heal. She had a longing to be back in Ireland and a burden to pray for the work there. Sadly, many of the reports she was getting back from Ireland were not encouraging.

The bookshop remained perpetually empty and the café was barren. Nasty rumors were being spread amongst the students that An Tobar Nua was a cult. One parent complained, "Anyone with prices that low is up to something. I don't like it." An Tobar Nua was neither exclusively Catholic nor Protestant. In a country where lines of religion were distinctly labeled, the ministry was making the hardliners uncomfortable. Outside of the occasional wandering tourist and a sprinkling of students, the café remained vacant. Many days, the staff played board games to relieve the boredom.

During that time, the staff felt both emotionally exhausted and spiritually overwhelmed. Though fully committed to the work, it was a discouraging time. The loss of Kelly and Susan's daily enthusiasm and encouragement left them unsure of new direction. Eamon was keeping the boat afloat, but water was flooding in through the cracks. During those dark months, no one knew if there was a future for An Tobar Nua.

But Susan was healing. In April of 1999, the doctor gave her a clean bill of health. The cancer was gone. Yet by the time the Currys talked of returning to Ireland a trusted friend in Ireland strongly suggested they not come back. They turned to the Lord for direction and discussed with their Board whether this counsel was from God. Cancer may have shaken them, but instead of throwing in the towel, with the Board's support, the Currys determined to return. They had tossed their hat over the wall. Nothing was going to hold them back.

At the end of April, seven months after Susan and the family left for the States, the Currys returned to Galway. A great joy erupted amongst the staff. Eamon felt the burden of leadership happily shared as Kelly and Susan returned spiritually charged. It was time for the troops to regroup and prepare for the future.

~

Everyone quickly adjusted to the school seasons. The café's year concluded in June as students finished up their exams before summer break. July became the month to retool, take a holiday, and train new volunteers who had committed for the upcoming school year. As they stepped back to regroup, Kelly, Susan and Eamon felt relieved to have survived An Tobar Nua's first year of existence.

Over the summer, it was decided that a few new items would be added to the menu, such as homemade scones, brownies, and fresh sandwiches. Youth music nights, Tuesday night Bible studies, off-the-wall games at lunch, and prize giveaways would be incorporated in year two. Everyone worked hard to improve what they were doing. When the new school year started in September, they were off and running full speed ahead.

But no matter what they did, the ups and downs in attendance continued. One week the café would pack out, and the next it was empty. Whenever they were discouraged, Eamon was a rock of encouragement. He would often say, "Just wait. The Irish have seen many people come and go. It'll take time. Stick it out." As a war history buff, Kelly knew that the key to an ultimate breakthrough in any battle was longevity. The staff needed to dig in and advance, even if the circumstances looked dire. The community needed reassurance that An Tobar Nua was here to stay and that there was no agenda but to serve joyfully and share the love of Christ freely. Building that kind of deep trust was going to take time.

The ministry and the Currys survived rumors, culture shock, and the Celtic Tiger. With the Lord's help, they and their team created a successful café in Galway with no prior experience in the restaurant business, avoided denominational infighting, and had even overcome cancer. The spiritual warfare was intense and their enemy was ruthless. But as long as they girded themselves with the Lord's armor and allowed Christ to be their Chieftain, they trusted He would complete His work.

―

The most powerful source of encouragement for the staff came whenever they saw a single life turn around. Tommy was one of the first. Raised in a Traveller community, Tommy was used to living as an outsider. The Irish Traveller subculture, roughly 5% of Ireland's population, traditionally follows a nomadic lifestyle comprised of a close knit community of families who maintain separate customs and culture. The Travellers live under a strong mistrust from the rest of Irish society. Often discriminated against, the Traveller community has become Ireland's outcasts.

Tommy came from a settled Traveller family from Galway City. He started visiting the café with his friend, Paddy, when he was 17 years old. Although raised culturally Roman Catholic, Tommy heard the gospel of Christ in a new way from a kind older woman, Philomena, when he was 13 years old. Philomena sowed the seed in Tommy's life, and then encouraged him to visit An Tobar Nua. There Kelly and the staff spent many hours watering that seed through encouraging conversations. Thinking back on that time, Tommy states, "It took many years to make a commitment to Christ, and I'm not sure I would have taken the leap of faith without the support and encouragement from An Tobar Nua. I had always felt drawn to Christ, but I also always said I'd give my life to him later. Kelly became my friend and I would spend hours asking him questions. Here was a group of guys and girls my age that served Christ and weren't weird. The staff at An Tobar Nua had something I wanted." Tommy became a regular at the café.

"Finally, in 2001, I had heard enough. One night, all alone in my bedroom, I asked Christ to come into my life. It was time to lay down roots. That night everything changed. Christ entered my heart."

~

Those like Tommy were the reason An Tobar Nua existed as a safe haven for the spiritually lost or those hungry for more of Christ. Long-term relationship was the key. All the staff had to do was give the Holy Spirit a place to stir hearts. God, and God alone, would draw the hearts of men and women to Him.

By the summer of 2000, two years after the doors first opened, the café was a community fixture. Students began to gather in droves at lunchtime and hang out during their free time. It was known as a safe place. Regardless of overwhelming circumstances, it appeared the Lord was moving in Galway and An Tobar Nua was an essential part of His plan.

Chapter 9

Momentum

*I will give you hidden treasures, riches stored in secret places,
So that you may know that I am the Lord, the God of Israel,
who summons you by name.*
Isaiah 45:3 (NIV)

*But you will receive power when the Holy Spirit
has come upon you, and you will be my witnesses in Jerusalem
and in all Judea and Samaria, and to the end of the earth.*
Acts 1:8 (ESV)

MIKE SHORTT'S LIFE MIGHT HAVE GONE in several different directions, but working with An Tobar Nua was not one he could have ever predicted.

Born in the turbulent city of Belfast during the Irish Troubles, Mike's family moved to the safer city of Shannon in the south of Ireland when he was a small boy. With its unpredictable streets, full of horrendous acts of violence between Protestants and Catholics, Belfast was no place to raise a family. Yet distance from the Troubles and having a faith-filled Catholic family did not prevent the anger that began to fill Mike's heart.

As he grew, Mike often rebelled against authority. He vented his frustration through heavy drinking and experimenting with drugs. He tried martial arts and brawling. One unfortunate young man who challenged Mike ended up in intensive care for three days with all his front teeth smashed in. Mike tried anything that might make him feel significant and in control. Eventually he ended up in court for his involvement with friends in the petrol bombing of an empty secondary school.

When Mike was 19 he moved to London, and here he became much more aware of his Irish-ness. He often visited The Four Provinces, a bookshop in Holborn. Here, he purchased books about the political situation in Northern Ireland written by the members of Sinn Féin, the political wing of the IRA at that time.

One particular book outlined the story of one of Mike's cousins who had escaped the infamous Maze, a prison in North Ireland that held political prisoners. Mike was filled with admiration for his cousin.

The more Mike read, the more he became filled with hatred against the British occupying army and British rule in North Ireland. Mike began to fantasize about blowing up the Houses of Parliament, killing politicians and soldiers. The IRA was determined to do whatever necessary, including terrorism, to free Ireland from the vestiges of English occupation.

But Mike's curiosity for the IRA was quelled when one of his friends back home was murdered in a club one night. This event contributed to Mike's contemplation about the meaning of life and how short it can be.

The 22-year-old still had an unquenchable need for meaning and purpose. His propensity toward violence, anger, and politics had left him frustrated and empty. He began to look for people in his life who seemed most fulfilled and at peace. Did he know anyone who understood real harmony and lived a life of meaning? As Mike pondered the question, he realized the answer would not be found from a historical figure or a famous athlete. People with riches, notoriety, or political power were as empty as he was. There was one person Mike knew who lived in perpetual peace and joy—his saintly grandmother. She was a woman of faith, of prayer, and of peace. Mike remembered back to a time when, as a young boy, he would pray with Granny. It was at this point in his adult life that Mike made the most dangerous decision possible. He prayed, "God if you are real, reveal yourself to me. Show me if I am significant. Show me if I matter. Show me what life is about."

Not long after his prayer, Mike was introduced to a group of Christians in London who were different than most he had known in his life. These 'Christ-followers,' like his grandmother, were not using their religion to push a political agenda nor were they simply Christian by birth. These were people his own age who found their significance in Jesus Christ. Their faith was expectant. Their faith was action. Mike's curiosity sparked long conversations with these Christ-followers about who Jesus was and who He was not. No one in history had been as radical, as committed, and as relevant as Christ. A day came when Mike accepted that the significance he longed for would only be found in Christ.

One night, after attending church, Mike prayed for a wife. Not long after he met Cathy. The 6' 4" dark-haired Irishman caught her eye and she agreed to go out with him. On their first date, they talked of their faith in Christ. Mike could not believe that he had met a beautiful Catholic girl who was bold in her faith and unashamed to live as a Christ-follower. Cathy was the girl of Mike's dreams. They began to pray, read the Bible, and attend Mass together.

As he worked and saved money, Mike began to read basic theology and learn about the Sacraments. He also revisited the Catholic Church of his youth, but this time he went with different eyes and different ears. The Mass became a source of strength. Yet something was still missing. Though his heart was aimed toward living a Christian walk, he felt powerless to live out that walk daily.

One night, while talking to Cathy, Mike began to share his struggle with flesh and spirit; obedience and disobedience; sin and righteousness. He explained that he felt powerless to walk as an obedient Christ follower, yet it was how he desired to live. Cathy told Mike about the power of the Holy Spirit. She explained that God longs to give us power to live a life of obedience. She shared a promise Jesus gave to his disciples: "'If you love me, you will keep my commandments. And I will ask the Father, and he will give you another Helper, to be with you forever, even the Spirit of Truth, whom the world cannot receive, because it neither sees him nor knows him. You know him, for he dwells with you and will be in you.'" (John 14:15-17 ESV). The Holy Spirit of God resided within Mike. All he had to do was ask the Spirit to fill him. Cathy then read him a passage out of Acts 1: "But you will receive power when the Holy Spirit has come upon you, and you will be my witnesses in Jerusalem and in all Judea and Samaria, and to the end of the earth." (Acts 1:8 ESV). As Cathy spoke of God's word, something stirred in Mike. "Cathy, will you pray with me? I need the power of God's Spirit in my life." Holding hands, the couple prayed.

Mike's own words best explain what happened in the seconds after they prayed. "I know this will sound strange, but I experienced a physical sensation of God's Spirit welling up within me. I literally felt God's unconditional love. So I responded. I began to pray, to weep, to acknowledge the Spirit of God in my heart. I remember waking up the next day feeling that same Presence surrounding me and I asked God to never leave me."

Over the next few months, Mike walked through the process of forgiving those who had wronged him throughout his life. As he attended various prayer groups, he found, in the Body of Christ, the acceptance he had always been seeking. Confession and the Eucharist, once dead rituals to an angry young man, became fountains of healing, strength, and love. A few months later, Mike and Cathy were joined in the sacrament of holy marriage.

By 1999, the Shortts had moved back to Ireland and they were a growing family. They relocated to the historic town of Athenry just outside of Galway. Mike was focused on establishing a life for his family, finding a place in his local church, and building his career. While working in Galway, Mike heard about a new Christian bookstore and café. The first time he walked into the café, he knew it was a special place. Every once in a while, he stopped in for tea or to pick up a book from the bookstore. It did not take long for Mike and Kelly to become fast friends. What impressed Mike the most about the café was the true ecumenical spirit that permeated the ministry. Those working at An Tobar Nua were not trying to convert anyone away from Catholicism. They focused on the love of Christ and they encouraged all their patrons to celebrate in the Christian church of their choice.

Mike began to meet the students that would come into the café. One such student was Adrian, who was attending Yeats College in Galway. Adrian began dropping in to An Tobar Nua looking for a bite to eat at lunch. He was impressed by the consistency of the staff's faith. He had been nominally Catholic but something about the spiritual depth, knowledge, and purpose of young people his own age piqued his curiosity. Adrian spent hours talking to the staff. It did not take him long to dive deeper into his Catholic roots and his Christian faith.

Stories like Adrian's warmed Mike's heart. For Mike, who had been traveling toward some very dark corners only a few years before, here was a place where people of different denominations focused on Christ and encouraged one another in their faith journeys. Mike recalled, "There was something special about this place and I had a sense that I needed to be a part [of it], but what that part was I had no idea." Mike began to attend Kelly's Bible study and keep his heart open to where the Spirit might lead him.

As the school season began in 2000, there were a lot of good things happening. Having Mike Shortt, a recognized Catholic lay leader in the Galway community, endorsing the shop helped quash the cult rumors. The lunch queues of students were winding out the door and down the block, even if the café was relatively quiet at other times. Kelly and Eamon barely kept up with the cooking frenzy in their tiny kitchen during the students' lunchtime. The food (especially the desserts) at the café was a success. And the one Friday night per month, reserved for concerts or game nights, brought an entirely different crowd into the café.

Students like Megan began to hang out regularly at the café. Megan attended a local Jesuit school. She had heard the rumors about the café and she decided to visit on her own to find out the reason for all the fuss. She soon learned it was a Christian café, and though she hadn't been raised in church, she was interested in learning what An Tobar Nua was about. Megan shared, "My first impression was how friendly the staff was to everyone. But I learned over time that the source of the An Tobar staff's joy was Jesus. I was a pretty shy girl but I asked a lot of questions, and they had intelligent answers. A bunch of us girls came to a faith in Christ that year. My journey to God began at An Tobar Nua."

To Kelly and Susan's delight, the staff was not only bonding but was adopting the vision as their own mission. Community was established among the team as they gathered at the Currys' home after church on Sunday afternoons to enjoy a meal, relax, laugh, and grow together. All the hard work and sacrifice was producing a bountiful harvest. Over time, the Sunday afternoon gatherings stretched beyond the staff as they invited others they had met through the coffee shop. It was a great time to deepen relationships and explore spiritual questions, while lasting friendships were forged.

~

One morning, inspired in prayer, Kelly told Susan he believed God was calling them to do a coat giveaway, but he was not sure "who" was to receive them. Many years prior, they had been part of a civic club in Kentucky that gave away hundreds of coats to disadvantaged inner-city children and youth as the cold winter approached. They discussed the idea of a coat giveaway but they were not aware of a specific need and they certainly could not pinpoint who the recipients should be.

At that time, a rapid social change was taking place in Ireland. The Irish government opened their doors to several African nations, allowing an influx of refugees unlike anything Ireland had ever experienced. For the first time ever, large numbers of Africans were making their way into a country that was 99% Caucasian. That decision would lead to a plethora of social challenges in the following years.

That fall, Susan was asked by their pastor's wife to attend a meeting that focused on how Irish citizens could help the African refugees. This was the first time the Currys heard that the government was beginning to send refugees to Galway. Most of the refugees were arriving in summer clothes, ill-prepared for the cold, damp Irish weather. The bleak winters were a challenge for locals, let alone a group of people moving in from a sub-Saharan climate. Susan returned home that evening and told Kelly that perhaps this was the "who" that his prayer was about.

With winter approaching, the staff immediately started a jacket drive. Obtaining the help of the local Social Welfare office and partnering with local businesses that gave the charity special prices, Foundation in Christ Ministries, Ltd., the parent charity that operates An Tobar Nua, began collecting coats. The Irish are some of the world's most generous givers, so it did not take long for sufficient financial donations to be given by those who wanted to help.

By December, the café seemed to hold most of Galway's coat and jacket supply. Many happy refugees weathered their first Irish winter in relative comfort and new and lasting friendships were born as a result of the coat drive.

An Tobar Nua continued to build momentum during the rest of the school year as the staff found their footing, and the café became a fixture in downtown Galway. By the summer of 2001, the café had its fourth set of volunteers. One of those volunteers, Ryan, had no idea that he would give the next six years of his life to the vision of An Tobar Nua. Ryan's tumultuous years as a teenager started coming to a close when, at 18 years of age, he surrendered his life to Christ. At 19, Ryan registered for Ravencrest's one-year Bible program, the same program Kelly and Susan had attended a few years prior. Toward the end of his time at the Bible school, Kelly came to visit the students and tell of the potential volunteer opportunities at the café.

Ryan remembered his first impressions of Kelly and the opportunity to join the An Tobar Nua team. "The first thing you notice about Kelly is his laugh. His laughter comes easily and is infectious. As I listened to him talk, it was his easy laughter that really caught my attention." In the days following Kelly's presentation, Ryan could not get the opportunity to serve at An Tobar Nua out of his mind. "I thought, 'What the heck, I'll turn in an application and see what happens.'"

In July of 2001, Ryan landed at Shannon Airport with no idea of what to expect. Ryan said, "I was eager, naïve, and looking for some sort of purpose. This was my first time out of America. When I landed in Ireland I didn't even know it was an island."

Other volunteers also came, hoping to make a small difference in the world. Kelly and Susan had to learn as much about leading a team of volunteers as they had learned about living with and serving the Irish. People skills were a must, and the life choices the staff made while in Ireland had a lasting effect on the ministry. Conflict had to be managed properly and in a Godly fashion. And every once in a while, staff members needed healing as much as those they were ministering to. Throughout the existence of An Tobar Nua, the volunteer program would bring both great joy and sometimes immense challenges. But without these volunteers there was no ministry.

Two more major changes happened in 2001. The bookstore in the back of the café seldom got much traffic. Many customers never even knew it was there. During her long months of cancer treatment in the States, Susan had told Kelly that she was praying for the shop next door to move so they could open a bookstore with a storefront. They had laughed at the improbability of such a miracle. The popular fish shop, Fleming's, did not appear to be departing any time soon. And it was a silly thought anyway, as they still were not fully utilizing the space they had.

In August, Kelly excitedly grabbed Susan and pulled her next door to see the sign on the front of Fleming's Fish Shop. Fleming's was moving. All of a sudden, Susan's prayer had become a reality. Contemplating a new lease at this time was mentally daunting. The café was not generating enough business to carry another piece of property. Though they had hoped for this answer to prayer, they had no expectation that the answer would come so fast.

After several months, when no one moved on the property, they took the risk and leased the space. The bookstore moved out from the back of the café, doubling their seating capacity, and into the new building. They converted the fish-scented space into one of the loveliest Christian bookstores in Ireland. Christians from every cloth enjoyed the selection of inspirational reading, music, and art at the newly christened Bóthar Emmaus Bookshop.

Kelly and Susan were praying desperately for others to join them in their work. They wanted to find more Irish people to join the staff. In particular, they knew the time had arrived to find someone who would support the ministry in a significant leadership role. But after months of searching, the hunt for an Irish person to join their management team was proving unfruitful. They searched throughout the country, but months of leads always led to dead ends, so they began looking for someone from the States. The direction was clear and they repeatedly prayed, "Lord, we need someone like Mike Shortt: an Irishman with an intense love for Christ and a heart to share God's love." Their deep respect for Mike had prompted them to invite him onto FICM's Board of Directors, and as they came to know him even better, their respect for his Christian integrity only deepened. He was an example of the leadership they needed.

As 2001 came to a close, Mike Shortt was helping lead *Life in the Spirit* seminars around Ireland. An evangelistic outreach of the Catholic Church, *Life in the Spirit* seminars teach about the presence and person of Jesus Christ, the journey of spiritual formation, and the power and reality of the Holy Spirit in the lives of Christ followers. Cathy and Mike prayed for clarity. He knew his time at his current job was coming to an end. And though he did not know what it was, he was sure Jesus had something very different in mind for his life.

Mike sought Kelly's advice about the call on his life. "I told Kelly I felt I was supposed to be an evangelist for Christ. I didn't know where or how but I knew I needed to pursue my call. Even with a growing family, I could no longer ignore the call on my life to full time ministry."

Kelly looked at Mike for a minute and then said, "Hey bud, you're already involved here. What about coming to work for An Tobar Nua?"

Mike smiled at God's leading. "All this time, the next step was right under my nose." He loved An Tobar Nua and their mission. He knew he was called to minister and longed to share Christ. Kelly and Susan had been looking for Irish management and leadership and Mike's gift of evangelism and heart for the Lord were undeniable. Mike accepted the job. Kelly jokingly said, "All the time we were praying, 'Lord, we need someone like Mike.' The Lord must have been sighing in exasperation and repeating over and over, 'Guys, it IS Mike!'"

Mike's gifts and his management skills were exactly what the Lord had planned. An Tobar Nua was becoming an Irish-led mission.

CHAPTER 10

A Good Harvest

*The least of you will become a thousand, the smallest a mighty nation.
I am the LORD; in its time I will do this swiftly.*
Isaiah 60:22 (NIV)

*But blessed is the one who trusts in the Lord,
whose confidence is in him. They will be like a tree planted by the
water that sends out its roots by the stream. It does not fear when
heat comes; its leaves are always green. It has no worries in a year of
drought and never fails to bear fruit.*
Jeremiah 17:7-8 (NIV)

BY THE FIFTH YEAR OF ITS existence, An Tobar Nua was stretching its wings. After Eamon's departure, Mike took over as the café manager. The Tuesday night Bible studies were well attended, and lunchtime every day was packed out. New volunteers came every July, bringing fresh voices and new life. Half of the staff was now Irish, which added to the excitement.

Tommy recounted how he applied for a position that year. "I literally had a dream I was working at An Tobar Nua. I felt silly but I decided to apply. I'd never worked at a ministry, but I did have a little restaurant experience. By this point, I had made it through Bible School, but I didn't think there was any way that Kelly would hire me. But that is the best part about An Tobar Nua. Sometimes the most unlikely people become a part of the team."

Even though times were good, the ferocity of spiritual warfare continued. Though they reaped great joy from serving, the staff had to remain vigilant in their prayers and personal devotionals. Each workday began with Bible study, prayer, or praise as a team. They knew that if they attempted to serve in their own strength, they could be crushed by the weight of the ongoing spiritual battles. Nothing was done without an undergirding of prayer.

As the student lunch crowd grew to lines out the door and down the street, Susan began training in Biblical counseling. When the time came for her to begin her practicum work, she found herself wrapped up with the day-to-day operations of the Bóthar Emmaus Bookshop. This amount of responsibility left little room for her to complete the necessary hours of counseling practice by the next year's course and besides that, she had no clients. Susan began to question if she should drop the course and asked the Lord to reveal His will. She was well aware that He would have to send the clients as well as someone to oversee the bookstore if she was to move forward with her training.

One day, Kathy Hegarty, a lovely young woman with a disarming smile and a soft Donegal accent, came into the café and asked if An Tobar Nua had any job openings. She had been praying about how to give herself to greater service for Christ when a friend had suggested that the café might be the perfect place for her. The most current need was in the bookstore, and although Kathy had no experience in sales, she clearly had deep-seated faith.

That kind of faith was the most important requirement for Mike and the Currys, so she joined the team. It did not go unnoticed that the Lord had provided the person they needed for the job, without even advertising the need, so that Susan could be freed up for counseling. Shortly afterwards, the Lord began to send in clients for Susan, and the counseling ministry began to develop.

A quick learner, Kathy did even better than they could have anticipated. The bookstore became her ministry, and the community instantly embraced this woman with a charming personality who put customers at ease. With a heart for intercession, she had a genuine concern for every person who walked through the door of the bookstore. People often shared their prayer needs with her. Many times,

Kathy would find herself praying with a stranger who wandered into the store out of curiosity, or she would refer the person for prayer with An Tobar Nua's prayer team. Within a year, Kathy transformed Bóthar Emmaus Bookshop into a quality bookstore as well as a safe place to find a listening ear and compassionate prayer.

After several years, Kathy left to follow a calling she had long prayed about and joined with the Dominican Sisters of Renewal, serving amongst the impoverished in New York City. She left, in her wake, a vibrant tradition of prayer ministry in the bookstore. Her replacement, Deirdre Morris, arrived shortly after.

Deirdre initially heard about An Tobar Nua's prayer ministry and arrived at the café to ask for intercession. She felt that the Lord was calling her to serve Him in ministry, yet her background was in merchandising. As the team began to pray that she would find a perfect fit for her skills, they realized she was exactly what they needed for the bookstore. She joyfully joined the team and Bóthar Emmaus Bookshop prospered under her prayerful leadership and great savvy for retail. Her heart to serve God translated into great service to those who came into the shop and the tradition of praying with customers continued.

―

After over half a decade, An Tobar Nua had weathered the ups and downs of pioneering a ministry. It had now become an established and healthy outreach. The time for bigger dreams came when a rare opportunity revealed itself in 2003.

Most of the schools in Ireland are Catholic and Religious Education is a regular course of study. A friend of Mike's, a local school teacher, had asked him to share his testimony with a classroom of secondary students. Mike had heartily accepted. After several classroom visits, he took young workers from the ministry into the classes to give their testimonies. The staff wanted to have a wider impact on the students in the community and this opportunity appeared to be an answer to prayer.

Around this time, the worldwide release of the movie *The Passion of the Christ* sparked Mike to draft a pamphlet explaining the core Gospel message in a uniquely Catholic context entitled *The Passion, Why?*. Originally written to pass out to café visitors, the pamphlet got into the hands of local priests who then also passed it on. Soon, people from other parts of Ireland, and even England, were calling to find out how they could get copies. A section of tables in the café became a staging area for boxing up pamphlets for shipments before opening times each morning. For the next two years, over 80,000 copies of *The Passion, Why?* became available in nearly every parish in Ireland. Thanks to the doors opened by this little pamphlet, An Tobar Nua was reaching the far corners of the Emerald Isle in ways they never imagined. And now their work began to expand in a new direction.

Using the interest ignited by the movie and Mike's pamphlet, the ministry rented a local movie theater for three private showings of *The Passion* to students from participating schools. In conjunction with this, Mike developed a retreat program focused on the apologetics for the Resurrection. Offering this opportunity to the teachers, Mike took a team from An Tobar Nua into the schools. As the students were enthusiastic, the invitations increased and the teachers encouraged more retreats.

The staff all felt, at first, that the prospect of visiting the schools was terrifying. "You never know what you might run into or what kind of questions the students would ask," explained Tommy. "Going into the schools is a challenge. We really have to know what we believe and why we believe it."

The following year, a new day-long retreat was developed, covering a variety of subjects, such as sexual purity, relationship with

Christ, and life choices from a Biblical perspective. Mike and the ministry staff rotated through the various presentations, with someone giving a personal testimony and a Gospel presentation each time. It was suggested that the students might enjoy the retreats even better if they were held at the café, away from school. The students spent the entire day at An Tobar Nua, with a snack break and lunch of their favorite menu items. That proved a great success and the café became a hangout for those students who had first visited for retreats.

In almost every case, the team connected with the students faster than they imagined. Their visits became fun and energizing. Before long, the team was leading retreats in seven schools and reaching hundreds of students. The schools and their students appreciated the well-thought-out and heartfelt responses of the team. Some of those students would find a special place at An Tobar Nua.

―

2004 was Megan's last year of secondary school. Through her continual visits to An Tobar Nua, Megan's walk with Christ matured. "The café provided the perfect foundation to grow in my journey with Jesus," she asserted. "The staff was a great source of friendship and encouragement in this journey." Like most of the students in her class, Megan pondered what her future held. She weighed the options of going the university route or taking a year off. During this time, Megan began to sense God leading her to work at An Tobar Nua. Serving at the café would be a radically different direction than the majority of her peers would take, but as the school year came to a close, Megan prayerfully decided to meet with Kelly to discuss joining the team.

In July 2004, Megan became the first person from the public schools to transition from student to staff at An Tobar Nua. In time, Megan grew in confidence, becoming a natural at building relationships and sharing God's love with students. During the next school year, the quiet introvert was sharing with hundreds of students at retreats in schools throughout County Galway about the good news of Christ. Megan was learning how to lead by serving others.

~

As 2005 began, Kelly and Susan began to dream again. Since their year of education at Ravencrest, the Currys believed in the benefits of a Scripture-based school, where students systematically learned God's Word and took practical ministry classes that prepared them to pursue their purpose in Christ. For years, An Tobar Nua had offered Bible studies, but Kelly and Susan both believed it was time for something bold and new. They wondered if they could run a credible, academically and spiritually exceptional Scripture school? Just like the choice to move to a foreign country, to start a café or to create a bookstore, the Currys had no practical experience in establishing a Scripture school, but obedience to God always brought surprising results.

The first step was to bring someone onto the team who had the necessary credentials. They prayed and hoped for someone highly educated, deeply spiritual, and exceptionally motivated in order to create a program from the ground up. This was a tall order to fill, and they thought they might have to settle for someone right out of graduate school. So when they received an email from Dr. Arden C. Autry inquiring about the position, Kelly thought someone was pulling a practical joke on him.

~

As a young man, Arden Autry was drawn to ministry. He also discovered he had a love for teaching. The journey to merging these passions began when Arden pursued higher education at Oral Roberts University in Tulsa, Oklahoma, where he graduated with a Bachelor of Arts degree in New Testament. He then attended Trinity Evangelical

Divinity School in Deerfield, Illinois, to obtain his Master of Arts in New Testament.

During his time at Trinity, Arden began a one-year internship at Logan Square Evangelical Free Church in Chicago. After his internship, his position at Logan Square turned into a full-time job and Arden became the pastor of the church for the next two years. He fondly recalled those precious years of pastoral ministry. "I loved preaching on Sundays and teaching my parishioners from the word of God. But the greatest realization I walked away with at Logan Square E-Free was that I was not called to pastoral ministry." In 1975, Arden and his wife June moved to Waco, Texas, so Arden could complete his PhD in New Testament at Baylor University.

The Autrys were back in Tulsa, Oklahoma, by 1978, where Arden was hired to teach Biblical Interpretation, New Testament Greek, and a selection of Bible classes at his alma mater ORU. For the next sixteen years Arden did what he loved: teaching the Word of God.

Their home church, First United Methodist Church of Tulsa, asked Arden to join their staff in 1994. They were looking for a Minister of Adult Learning and they could not imagine anyone who was more qualified or a better fit than Arden. It was a big decision to leave ORU, where Arden was a tenured professor. On the other hand, Arden loved teaching at the church, which he had been doing on a voluntary basis since 1980. After much prayer, he decided to make the move from ORU to First UMC of Tulsa.

First UMC of Tulsa was the kind of place that the Autrys could call home. Arden and June were comfortable there. They were fulfilled as they were working hard, being diligent, and walking in God's call. They developed deep roots and created a safe, stable, satisfying life. So when Arden told June he was getting restless, she was worried. Administrating a large education program for a mega-church was wearing him thin. Arden missed the fun of teaching every day and the satisfaction of watching young students grow in their faith. And though Arden loved his teaching role in the church, he felt it was time for a change. June wondered how her self-described 'risk averse' husband could contemplate changing the direction of his life. "Arden is normally a settled person and I thought his restlessness would pass," said June. "Certainly we were not going to make any major changes in the prime of our lives. Boy, was I wrong."

To celebrate their 35th anniversary, Arden and June planned a holiday to Ireland. When a former colleague and close friend at ORU, Dr. Jim Shelton, heard Arden was going to Ireland, he suggested they visit An Tobar Nua to see what Kelly was doing. Dr. Shelton brought Kelly into his class every year to share the vision of the ministry with his students. In a country infamously known for its sectarianism, An Tobar Nua had both Catholics and Protestants ministering side by side. He thought Arden might want to witness a place of healing and ecumenical harmony. Arden stored the idea in the back of his mind. His focus was on a relaxing getaway with June.

On May 1, 2005, Arden and June departed from Chicago O'Hare to the sound of the Irish pipes and the rhythm of the bodhrán as American Airlines was celebrating their new direct flight to Ireland. For the next couple of weeks, the Autrys traveled throughout the island, enjoying verdant landscapes, grey-stone monuments, and the most hospitable people on the planet. Ireland was everything they imagined and more. They pulled into Galway on a Friday evening and it took a fair bit of exploration to locate An Tobar Nua. By the time they arrived, the café was closed. There was no one around to talk to, so Arden took a peek in the windows. Walking along the canal next to the café, he noticed some sort of construction was underway.

"An Tobar Nua looked interesting," said Arden, "but when no one was there to show us around, we decided to hit the road again. I never really thought another thing about it." The Autrys enjoyed the rest of their holiday and then returned home to Tulsa. "When I got home, I couldn't get the building out of mind," Arden continued. "I kept wondering what they were building. So I decided to go onto their website to get an answer."

The information he found was very different than what he was seeking. As he clicked through the Foundation in Christ website, he came across an advertisement looking for someone to help pioneer a Scripture school in Galway. Intrigued by the possibility, Arden emailed Kelly asking him about the courses he was hoping to offer. When Arden received Kelly's response, he was astonished: Old Testament and New Testament Survey, Romans, Hebrews, The Gospel of Christ, Apologetics for the Resurrection. The specific courses Kelly listed were Arden's areas of expertise.

"June, I think they may be looking for me."

June shook her head. "I don't think so." She certainly did not anticipate that Arden, who was in his mid-50s, would contemplate such a radical prospect at this time in their lives.

Still, Arden sent in his resume to Kelly. If this was what God had in store, Arden would soon know. Kelly received the application and scanned Arden's experience, education level, and impressive qualifications. Kelly immediately thought that Arden's resume was too good to be true.

Kelly was ecstatic when he followed up with Arden and the connection between the two men was instant. Kelly told Arden that he was going to be in Tulsa in a few months. They scheduled a dinner meeting so they could talk more.

In September of 2005, Kelly sat down with Arden and June. He shared, in detail, his hopes and dreams for a Biblical training center. As the conversation came to a close, Kelly soberly shared all the reasons the Autrys should not come to Ireland. Kelly believed the Autrys were the couple for the job, but he also wanted them to clearly understand how tough the endeavor would be and the spiritual, emotional, and mental challenges the couple would face if they came. Instead of being frightened, June and Arden were refreshed by Kelly's candor and the integrity of the ministry as a whole. Later, their pastor suggested the couple visit Galway to see if there was genuine chemistry between the organization and them.

With the prayers of their pastor, Arden and June visited An Tobar Nua in November 2005. The Autrys connected with the staff with ease. Brainstorming with them revealed the height of the challenges that lay ahead. The biggest question was how to get students to join the program. Mike Shortt sat down with Arden, advising him not to underestimate how hard starting a Scripture school would be in the west of Ireland. He and June needed to weigh the cost and only come if the Lord was leading. When the Autrys flew back to Tulsa, they had the weight of the decision on their shoulders.

As Dietrich Bonhoeffer wrote, "When Christ calls a man to Himself, He bids him come and die." Arden and June knew that if they made this move, then a part of them, their stable world, their risk-averse lives, and the comfort of their current community would die.

Chapter 11

Monumental Shifts

Then their eyes were opened and they recognized Him...
They asked each other, "Were not our hearts burning within us
while He talked with us on the road and opened the Scriptures to us?
Luke 24:31-32 (NIV)

The Sovereign Lord is my strength;
He makes my feet like the feet of a deer,
He enables me to tread on the heights.
Habakkuk 3:19 (NIV)

WHILE THE MINISTRY BEGAN TO DEEPEN its roots and branch out, another substantial change for An Tobar Nua had been quietly simmering in the background. For several years, the ministry had kept its eye on the building next door that housed their leased bookstore space on the ground floor. Although the building had been sold, its upper floors were still vacant. After the new owners' failed attempt to get a permit to use the space as a guest house, the building was once again on the market. But rising property prices and the condition of the building made acquisition of it nearly impossible.

Aside from the high list price, the structural integrity of the building was worrisome because of dangerous joist issues. The walls were slowly bending, causing the floors to rest six inches lower than where they were originally built. But the building could not be gutted because it was registered as a protected historical landmark. Windows, fireplaces, shutters and all original design odds and ends legally had to be preserved. Even the original style of painting had to be incorporated in the final design. An architect from the Historical Society's Preservation of Buildings Department would be required onsite to approve any changes. All the necessary codes and preservation requirements automatically added at least 20% to the cost of renovation. But, when the building once again went on the market, this time for auction, the Board was ready to move forward.

Despite all the challenges, cost increases, and months of interruption, everyone believed this move was God's will for the future of the organization.

Even with the Board's support, the agreed-upon maximum bid that they could offer was well below what they expected the building to sell for at auction. But God knew that they needed the space to expand, and on July 19, 2002, they won the auction.

―

With the purchase, An Tobar Nua's square footage could now more than triple in size, making room for expanding ministries, growing staff needs and a future Scripture school. With the approved planning in the late summer of 2004, renovations of the newly acquired property started in January of 2005 with a series of complex challenges.

Much to everyone's relief, Cormac Murphy, An Tobar Nua's original contractor, came back on the job. Cormac had to find a way to strengthen the foundation, preserve the historical integrity of the building, and seamlessly tie everything together with the original structure next door. The goal was to make the building's façade look like it did when it was first built. Not only did Cormac love the challenge, but he also rested in the peace of knowing more prayers would go into this project. He looked forward to seeing how God would work on their behalf. Cormac shared about his desire to take on the project. "One of the reasons I wanted to work with An Tobar Nua again was I saw the reality of changed lives. Over the years, since I had worked with them, I saw young lads like Tommy, Eamon, and Megan transform. In the beginning, I used to wonder why they came to be a part of this little café, but years later I could see the results. Their faith, whatever their particular church background, was deepened." Cormac had a soft place for Kelly. "I didn't know why this man, who obviously could succeed and make a lot of money elsewhere, wanted to be in Galway doing this. But I knew the man that brought holy water to pray over the building was a man of integrity, of faith and he loved what he was doing."

Kelly knew that Cormac, a man with common sense and integrity, understood their current needs, the building codes, and the specific requirements the ministry had for future growth.

―

Almost immediately, the building crew was discovering ingenious ways to solve their complex problems. Hidden treasures, such as detailed original flooring, stone walls, timber-framed windows and historic shutters, were uncovered and restored to their former beauty. In what would become more downstairs seating area, the workers found metal rings used for tying up horses in the stone walls that had once been the outer carriage house connected to the dwelling. And just outside, in an arched entrance into the yard, a hand-etched cross was discovered in the stonework - a sign that believers may have dedicated this building to the Lord. In fact, the woman whose grandfather had originally built the building had lived there until her 80s. Her niece later said that her aunt had hoped the building might one day be a building dedicated to prayer.

Though the remodeling process took ten months, the significance of the expanded meeting space would be revealed almost immediately. God's plans were beyond the desires and prayers of the staff. And those divine plans were made clear through a phone call to Kelly at the beginning of the New Year. In January of 2006, Arden contacted Kelly to tell him they were on board to join An Tobar Nua.

―

With the grand opening of the new building in August of 2006 came a new set of volunteers from America and the Autrys arriving to minister alongside the regular Irish staff. A year before, a new bishop was appointed in Galway. With his deep love of the Bible, he agreed to visit An Tobar Nua and to speak to various student and Bible study groups. With favor from the Bishop, opportunities multiplied for the retreat team in the upcoming school year.

By the fall, the retreat team was starting to engage in day retreats. Full day retreats allowed for expanded times of testimony and increased interaction with the students. The retreat team enjoyed talking to the students and they discovered their rhythm as a team. As the building tripled in size, state-of-the-art teaching spaces were created, allowing more school retreats to come to the building. This gave the team a more effective way to meet the needs of the students.

Along with the renovations came shifts and expansions in the responsibilities of leadership. At that time, Mike became the operations manager and outreach supervisor as the school retreats continued to expand in scope and number.

One of the blessings of refurbishment was the addition of onsite living space for some of the staff and a dorm area for Scripture school students. Seating in the café doubled, bringing increased business into the café and bookstore. Free Wi-Fi drew a larger university crowd. More outreach into the community resulted in a weekly small group, Lectio Divina, praise nights, and teaching seminars in the new classroom spaces. It was a challenging yet rewarding season as management dynamics matured. Focus shifted as An Tobar Nua transformed from a small mission outreach into an ecumenical Christian community center.

Breda McDonough explained that time well. "Galway needed something alongside of the church. An Tobar Nua [is] a place free from denominational strife. There are Catholics who model what it means to walk with Christ. There are Christians from various backgrounds that focus on the Risen Savior above all else. Respect, tolerance, common orthodoxy, healing, joy, delight—these are some of the words that describe the heart of An Tobar Nua. When we all dance together in heaven, we will be one. Jesus told us to be one. An Tobar Nua strives to obey that command. An Tobar Nua is Galway's safe place for the children of God. An Tobar Nua is a safe place for those who did not know what they believe. It is a place to experience God's love even if you do not believe in God."

Arden and June were the first couple to move into one of the new flats built during the latest construction, which had been prayerfully prepared for them. The couple quickly transitioned into the Irish way of life. Galway was an easy place to love. They spent the rest of the summer creating a game plan for the launch of the Emmaus Scripture School. There were several things to consider. They needed to attract students. Also, an entire curriculum had to be developed to meet the unique needs of the school, which would include both Irish and international students who would range in age from 18 to retirement age. Courses would need to be created for both credit and audit.

Some ministries were for particular periods of time. One of these was *Bridges*, a crisis pregnancy program which operated between the years 2006 and 2008, under the leadership of Anne Buckley. In partnership with a crisis pregnancy organization in another town and a visiting doctor, *Bridges* provided counseling and support to women experiencing unexpected pregnancies, as well as an ultrasound on a portable sonogram unit. The sonogram provided a 3-D image of the baby, and the unit was one of only three such machines in Ireland at the time, with the other two located in hospitals. When Anne left to pursue further education in chaplaincy work, it was the opportune time to combine the work with the ministry partner for greater effectiveness. While counseling was still provided as needed, the portable unit's use was expanded to many more locations around the country, including Galway.

The staff had learned over the years that the most important aspect of any ministry in Ireland was the formation of authentic relationships. If the Scripture school could not convince potential students that genuine community was possible while studying Holy Writ, then there would be no school. Kelly and Susan, years before, had experienced community at Ravencrest in Colorado and it was that particular sense of community that they desired to foster through Emmaus Scripture School.

In the fall of 2006, before there were any classes or students, Arden visited local churches, inviting their congregations to send parishioners to the Scripture school so that they could develop their ministry gifting within their communities. On Tuesday evenings, the Bible study program gave Arden an opportunity to teach until the January 2007 launch of the Emmaus Scripture School. All in all, Arden found the process invigorating. His Biblical scholarship, educational training, and years serving the body of Christ were coming to fruition in the development of the Scripture school. Looking back, he sat in wonder at God's sovereignty and the twists and turns that obedience to God brings in the life of those who dare to follow His lead. June's gentle, Godly spirit for prayer was shared when she began to lead a Saturday morning Lectio Divina group. Clearly the couple was an added blessing to the team and to the city.

―

The next couple of years brought steady growth in ministry ability and a greater depth of spiritual effectiveness. Those who had been with An Tobar Nua for years moved into positions of increased responsibility. The school retreats expanded into several successful retreats, such as *Romance without Regrets: A Study in Biblical Purity*, *Stoned Now - Wasted Later: Living a Substance-Free Life*, and *Questions of Faith*. There were lessons in leadership and adjustments to the growing crowds. With the growth came a demand for more volunteers, but the development of the Scripture school remained a primary focus during these years.

~

In January of 2007 the first semester of the Emmaus Scripture School officially launched with a freshman class of three people: an Eastern European immigrant and two Irish students. Those faithful three engaged as if they were in a class of three hundred. As the twelve-week term progressed, Arden assessed the pace, adjusting it subtly to shape the best experience for current and future students.

The stories of several of the students are inspiring. One student who enrolled in one of the early semesters was born into a Muslim family in a Middle-Eastern country. Through a series of hardships, she became a follower of Christ. The story of how she came to Ireland is both heroic and sad, but it was a matter of survival for her. When she learned about the Scripture school, she met with Arden to ask if she could enroll. Arden was concerned at first because she spoke with halting English and had almost no educational background. As a single mom, she struggled just to make ends meet. But Arden saw her determination and profound faith. He told her she could join classes as an audit student so that she would not have to complete any assignments or exams. Arden was stunned when she grabbed and kissed his hand. She was going to learn about Jesus and her joy was uncontainable. Inspired by her story and commitment, donations came in to cover her tuition through scholarship. Her enthusiasm and joy were present every time she came to class. Arden said, "I'll always remember her deep gratitude for this opportunity."

Since that humble beginning, the Emmaus Scripture School has managed to carve out a place for itself in Galway. In addition, many of the students are not Irish. For a variety of reasons, these students relocated to Galway from England, the USA, Switzerland, Ghana, South Africa, and other countries across the globe and later found a place at the Scripture School. The students are both Catholic and Protestant, an unusual situation in Ireland. Most of the students are simply seeking the opportunity to dive deep into Scripture and do not plan on pursuing a degree. But for those working toward further study and a degree, the credit often carries over to Christian universities. Over the years, the Emmaus Scripture School has evolved by creating a unique curriculum designed with a Celtic rhythm. And as its students have continued to mature in the word, ministry depth has expanded.

Arden and June handed the Scripture school over to John Shelton, an American pursuing his PhD from the London School of Theology, and his wife Grace, in 2010. Arden said of the impact of the school, "We are a good presence in the Galway Christian community. Every semester, we reach more Irish and international students. Our leadership is solid and Emmaus has become a safe place for both Catholics and Protestants. I believe the ripple effect will be felt through eternity."

Chapter 12

Back to Egypt

A promise they have from the Lord of hosts that He will break the yoke they bear when that day comes and part their chains asunder. No more shall they be at the mercy of alien masters; they shall obey the Lord their God only...
Jeremiah 30:8-9 (Knox)

Father, if you are willing, remove this cup from me. Nevertheless, not my will, but yours, be done.
Luke 22:42 (ESV)

ON FRIDAY, MAY 18, 2007, SUSAN sat down with a heavy heart and wrote in her journal: *Why downcast O my soul? The ups and downs of struggling with this decision, already made, but how hard the going forward is. I can see wisdom, yet I keep returning to the fact that maybe we are not trusting enough. We have repeatedly asked You to close the door but You did not. How I wished You would. We didn't want this. It blindsided us both.*

After the grand opening of the new building in August 2006, Kelly and Susan sensed a significant shift on the horizon. With the growth of the ministry came ever-increasing costs. More members of qualified staff were needed. The expansion meant the building would be open to the public for long periods of time, increasing utility demands. Materials, meals, technical equipment, printing, and development costs—all these details were necessary to meet the bigger demands.

These were welcome challenges for the ministry because it meant that more people were hearing about and experiencing the good news of Jesus Christ, and no one on staff complained about the opportunities to share God's love across the nation. One of the remarkable financial realities of the ministry was the increased contribution from the café and bookstore. What was once a financially

CHAPTER 12. Back to Egypt • 155

tight venture had become a budgetary ballast for the organization. By 2007, the café and the Bóthar Emmaus Bookshop were covering 40% of the annual budget. Compared with many non-profits, this was a tremendous victory, but there was still a 60% deficit for ever-expanding ventures and the staff needed to cover new programs.

Kelly, who understood the financial challenges of the organization better than anyone, started spending an increasing amount of effort in the U.S. raising funds. Adopting the model used by most mission organizations, Kelly visited potential donors and communicated the vision of An Tobar Nua in small gatherings. Unfortunately, the traveling, which involved several extended trips to the U.S. each year, did not produce a significant return on his investment of time and resources. The effort required to fundraise, along with the amounts needed, was continuing to grow as the ministry grew.

As the months rolled on, the financial pool remained shallow and Kelly began to grow frustrated with the traditional model of missionary fundraising. He started to feel like David attempting to wear Saul's armor into his battle with Goliath. He knew there had to be a more efficient way to raise support.

~

An opportunity opened up with Kelly's employer from 12 years ago. The company asked Kelly to act as a consultant for a few months. This seemed a win-win scenario for the organization. Kelly would be compensated for his consulting work and the money could be put toward the organization. In addition, the company would pay for his travel to company sites throughout the U.S. which meant that, with proper coordination, Kelly could create a simultaneous fundraising itinerary that matched his consulting schedule and defray the cost of travel. After talking and praying through the opportunity with the FICM board, the decision was made. Although Kelly would be doing double-duty, he knew a short season of work would bring a significant boost to the economic realities of the organization.

～

Toward the end of the fall, as Susan and Kelly assessed the budget for the upcoming year, they came to a tough realization. Kelly's consulting was underwriting most of the remaining budget, while the time Kelly spent knocking on doors to raise funds yielded far less. It looked as though more fundraising could not sufficiently cover the significant ministry deficit and the consulting job was only temporary.

～

As 2007 began, the couple wondered and prayed what their next move should be. There was another factor outside of fundraising that weighed heavy on Kelly's mind. Though Ireland's Celtic Tiger economy was in full swing, he was beginning to sense signs of an upcoming economic slowdown in the U.S. Kelly had studied the ebb and flow of world economies. Knowing the financial signs of the times were part and parcel of what he had done most of his life. If the U.S. slipped into recession, Kelly believed it was only a matter of time before the heavily credited Irish economy would follow suit and burst under the stress of business and personal debt.

If a worldwide recession were to come, An Tobar Nua, along with other ministries, would face challenges many people could not comprehend. Fundraising, especially in the U.S., would become even more difficult. Susan listened to Kelly's concerns, but the signs were not readily evident to her. And yet she had learned to trust that the Lord guided Kelly for the needs of the ministry. Looking ahead, the possibility of scaling back ministry outreach and reducing staff was a real possibility. But how could they consider doing either when the ministry was growing?

The thought of laying off people or cutting ministries was unthinkable. An Tobar Nua now had a strong base of Irish employees who loved their jobs and did them well, and new opportunities for ministry kept coming. They chose to believe the Lord would make a way of escape.

The next January, Kelly's boss from the company he was consulting for gave him a call. The company felt his consulting work had been helpful and they asked if he would come back full-time. To say that Kelly and Susan were flabbergasted was an understatement.

On one hand, the salary they offered Kelly would underwrite the budget necessary for An Tobar Nua's current needs and would avoid the difficulties of fundraising in a harsh economic climate. Kelly would also be doing something he excelled at. But there were an equal number of pressing issues on the other side of the argument. How would the ministry, which was co-founded by Kelly, operate without his presence? Would the staff feel cut-off or, worse, abandoned? What if Kelly's departure became counter-productive?

For Susan, the choice was agonizing. She had just completed her counseling diploma and her client base was growing. If she went back to the States with Kelly it would mean moving away from those people along with the workers they had grown to love. And while they had a wonderful staff, the increased load on everyone would be heavy. As an example, Mike Shortt could take over administration, but it would require him to cut back on retreat work.

It became evident that the only way it might work would be for Susan to split her time between supporting her husband in the U.S. and being in Ireland to support the staff during this major transition. But how would weeks of separation affect them? Were there enough people on staff to cover the greater responsibility? Kelly asked for thirty days to think and pray over the decision and the company graciously agreed.

The FICM board members were the first people they went to for wisdom and prayer. Several of them brought up the same questions that were stirring in Kelly and Susan's minds, along with more practical concerns about such an extreme decision. Initially, some of the board members were hesitant as there were outstanding issues that they could not wrap their minds around. They worried that Kelly's absence would backtrack the ministry, and it certainly was not the traditional way of approaching ministry funding. In the end, everyone agreed to a season of prayer to seek God's wisdom in the matter.

~

In early spring, the Currys took a family holiday for a chance to get away, fast and pray. By this time they had shared the possibility of the job with a few people. Many of them were positive, while others voiced the questions they had already been asking themselves: did they trust God to provide, or was this a distraction to take Kelly away from the ministry he'd given everything to pioneer? Kelly knew that without both Susan's and the entire Board's agreement, he would not make the move, no matter the financial benefits. Kelly loved the ministry and the people he worked with. A far cry from the man of many years ago, the thought of going back into the business world was not his first choice. But in the end, all he and Susan could pray was, "Thy will, not our will, be done."

During this time, Kelly helped a small church in Kentucky rework a bond issue that threatened the loss of their church building. Pastor Paul, a retired minister on the board of the church, watched as Kelly was able to help them navigate their financial and legal labyrinth and find a solution. Kelly's background in finance helped them tackle issues that were overwhelming to the leadership. His giftedness for business and his love for the people of God gave him an ability few leaders have in the realms of both ministry and business.

When the church was in order, Pastor Paul made a comment, completely unaware of the heavy decision weighing on Kelly and Susan. He said that he knew God had called Kelly to Ireland but he did not feel that God was finished with him in the business realm. He observed that God's kingdom needed workers with his skills and he wouldn't be surprised if the Lord led him to a place to use his gifting in financial administration. Could the Lord be using others to confirm the way He seemed to be leading?

During the season of prayer and fasting, one of the FICM board members had shared a profound thought. He felt that God might be moving Kelly back to the corporate world the same way He had taken Joseph to Egypt. Even though it felt like captivity, God brought Joseph to Egypt, as a slave, to prepare His people for a devastating famine that lay on the horizon. Could God be intending this job for a similar need? Through much prayer and discussion, it seemed the Lord was leading Kelly to take the position and the board was in agreement, though inwardly Susan still struggled. She had learned to trust that the Lord would lead them, but the price seemed high.

In May, Susan was struck by a chapter she opened in the Old Testament. Reading the Knox Bible, an older translation she seldom used, she turned to Jeremiah 30, a chapter she did not know well. But this morning she found herself drawn deep into the verses written 2700 years ago. Every word spoke to the questions that had been swirling around her head for months. Verses 8-10 made the strongest impact: "A promise they have from the Lord of Hosts that He will break the yoke they bear when that day comes and part their chains asunder. No more shall they be at the mercy of alien masters; they shall obey the Lord their God only…"

Susan thought back to when they first arrived in Ireland. Who would have ever imagined the spiritual warfare and struggles they would face? It was certainly a good thing that they had no idea of the challenges and battles they would face. If they had known, they might never have come. They had always felt the ministry needed to become Irish-led and though they had been sent for a time, they were still not Irish. An Tobar Nua needed to be a ministry directed and run by Irish leadership. God was developing the Irish to reach the Irish. The Lord seemed to be moving them in the direction of handing over leadership. Was now the time for Kelly and Susan to begin to move aside? Could they truly not be afraid and trust that the Holy Spirit was the One directing them to take this step?

Susan continued to read the verse. "Have then no fear, the Lord says, Jacob thou art my servant still. From that far country of exile I mean to restore thee, restore thou children of thine, ...have no fear, I am at thy side, the Lord says, to protect thee." God would take care of the details and there would still be work for them to do. They were to trust and not be fearful. Their biggest prayers were coming to pass.

The answer was clear. Reluctantly, yet wholeheartedly, Susan accepted God's will. Kelly was going back to work in the U.S.

No one realized that, when Kelly started his new position, the world was on the knife's edge of a four-year recession and that Ireland was about to go through its worst financial crisis in the modern history.

The recession was devastating to thousands of non-profits. People did not have the income to give as freely as before. Giving to churches and non-profits fell drastically, causing ministries around the world to crumble or pare down to bare bones just to survive. When Ireland sunk under one of the worst economic collapses in Europe, people started losing their jobs, losing their homes and losing their hope. The Celtic Tiger was dead.

Kelly prospered in his new job, helping secure the budget of An Tobar Nua throughout the recession. Not one staff member was let go. In fact, new staff were added as ministry opportunities opened up. In the midst of desperate economic times in Ireland, the staff remained peaceful.

The corporate world was a tough environment. Kelly faced incredible challenges in a business that was going through rapid change. Yet he remained faithful to the direction given to him by God. He ended up working for six years, helping the ministry build a fund that could meet the shortfall in the budget from the decline in donations over several years. Susan kept up a rigorous schedule of travel between Ireland and the U.S. and Kelly also made periodic visits to Galway to encourage, advise, and connect with those who continued in the work.

An Tobar Nua still required generous, God-directed donors, and still does today, but the ministry was able to weather the recession and expand. Kelly's six years of service achieved what more than years of traditional fundraising might have accomplished, making FICM and An Tobar Nua an anomaly in the world of non-profits.

Looking back, Kelly and Susan marvel at the wisdom of God that prompted them to trust Him even when the path of obedience was too blurry to see. Finishing out her journal entry that day in May, Susan wrote, *Lord, I don't know or understand the way forward except one step at a time. You alone must lead. I do know this is the time for the ministry to grow and expand, not shrink. Lord, let me be Your servant now and always.*

As He always proved, God provided exceedingly and abundantly above all that they had asked or thought.

In Conclusion

…but Not the End

*Observe therefore all the commands I am giving you today,
so that you may have the strength to go in
and take over the land that you are crossing the Jordan to possess.*
Deuteronomy 11:8 (NIV)

*When you performed awesome deeds that took us by surprise,
you came down, and the mountains trembled before you.
Since ancient times no one has heard or perceived,
no eye has seen any God besides you,
who intervenes for those who wait for him.*
Isaiah 64: 3-4 (NET)

AS THE WORLDWIDE RECESSION MADE ITS way across Ireland, An Tobar Nua continued to move forward with a renewed sense of purpose and passion. For a season, Kelly worked full-time in the States while Susan continued part-time in Ireland. But eventually, both Kelly and Susan were committed to work in the U.S. to raise the necessary capital (both financial and human) that kept the ministry in full swing. Mike Shortt took over as managing director, securing the original goal of Irish leadership within the organization. Today, as it has throughout the last twenty years, An Tobar Nua continues to shine as a beacon of light on the west coast of Ireland.

The outreach programs, such as Lectio Divina gatherings and Emmaus Scripture School, continue to challenge people to dive into God's Word and experience what it means to hear His voice. Passion Retreats in local secondary schools focus on the apologetics behind the life, death, and Resurrection of Christ. Follow-up discipleship classes for spiritual growth and practical classes on how to share your faith continue to grow in scope and impact. Many of these modes of ministry prepared the staff for a one-of-a-kind event that came to Galway in the summer of 2009.

From July 4 to July 19, Catholic lay leaders hosted one of the most exciting local events in decades. Creideamh (pronounced cred-jiv), a faith festival that focused on the good news of Jesus, was held in

Galway. After a year of preparation, the festival featured national and international speakers in venues throughout the city. A gazebo for prayer was set up in Eyre Square, the city's main park. A plethora of events took place day and night. The arts were represented through concerts, practical projects, café discussion, and street outreaches. Teams of Christians, both Catholic and non-Catholic, from across Ireland and other countries came to participate in this giant celebration of God's love.

An Tobar Nua became an integral part of Creideamh, both in the planning and as a special event location for speakers and other happenings. For the staff of the ministry, Creideamh was an outward sign that the growing spiritual atmosphere in Galway could affect the whole nation.

One of Susan's initial concerns as she eventually began spending more time in the States was the increasing demand for counseling at An Tobar Nua. Her counseling client base was growing at the time of her departure and she thought leaving might mean that that season was over for the ministry. But instead, it was only the beginning of a grander vision. Tommy and Megan, both who had been with the staff several years, began work to complete their four-year degrees in counseling. Their time at An Tobar Nua had solidified their calling as counselors.

Since its inception, the counseling ministry primarily grew each year by word of mouth. Christians and non-Christians alike continue to come to find healing, solace and wisdom in their emotional and spiritual struggles. Counseling, though professional, is donation based. Approximately half of the clients pay something. The ministry underwrites whatever else is necessary to maintain its standards of excellence.

Tommy has developed a specialty in suicide prevention. In workshops and throughout several Irish schools, he is asked to present talks that imbue hope for those who feel like life is not worth living. A counseling career is a reality Tommy would have never seen in his life as a young man. He is a testament to what Jesus and a loving community can do in the life of a young person seeking truth. Both Megan and Tommy continue to develop and expand the counseling ministry. Their days full of clients are also days filled with the joy of knowing they are making a difference.

The Café remains the platform where contact most often begins. As the ministry has grown and various outreaches require more specialization, the Café also benefits from a management team solely dedicated and focused on its operations. The relationships that develop within the Café, in afternoon programs with students, and evenings with adults complement the other branches of the ministry. In 2013, Jimmy Earle joined the team as Café manager, along with his wife, Meilyn. Bringing fifteen years of previous experience in evangelistic youth work, and also trained in the hospitality industry, Jimmy added a fresh perspective to the Café and volunteer program. Through encouraging and managing the team in the Café and the events taking place there, creativity has broadened in scope and depth. New methods and marketing strategies are explored in order to better serve the community.

Leadership continues to develop and deepen in effectiveness as different staff members exercise their talents, often by trying on several hats during their first few months on staff. In time, their natural gifts emerge, and they become leaders of a current ministry or create new ones to meet the growing needs of a rapidly changing world. The majority of these leaders are Irish, but there are still volunteers from around the world who join for a few weeks, months, or years to help with various areas in the ministry. These volunteers come from a multitude of Christian backgrounds with the goal of being unified in the message of Christ's love. An Tobar Nua endures as a beautiful example of a truly Christ-centered ecumenical community.

As the staff has grown, new methods of outreach have emerged. Some of the staff teach Alpha, an evangelistic course used throughout the world, that introduces seekers to the basics of Christianity and the meaning of life through open conversations. Discussions take place at local schools and in the café. Hundreds of students continue to take part in the school retreats, which are subject driven, filled with fun games, Scripture study, reflections, apologetics, and include, of course, a delicious meal. The Emmaus Scripture School, founded in 2006, has a steady stream of enthusiastic students who are learning the Bible through college-level courses. The Word of God is truly not returning void.

Various groups continue to meet in the café, including discipleship gatherings led by An Tobar Nua staff, impromptu study groups, faith-based community clubs, and summer youth camps. Today, the café covers about 30% of the total ministry budget while providing tasty desserts, affordable delicious meals, and what some say is the best cup of coffee in Galway. The regulars come several times a week, and any new faces that come through the front door are quickly greeted by friendly employees who buzz around the café serving the patrons. They may be busy, but they are never so rushed as to miss a chance to stop and dive into a good conversation. Every once in a while, one might even catch a surprise concert or join a night of praise and worship.

―

Kelly and Susan continue in their commitment to An Tobar Nua by offering their time and encouragement through mentorship, and along with their board, through strategic planning and developmental direction. Although the day-to-day operations of the ministry is in Irish hands, they continue to be intimately involved in the life of the ministry.

~

In 2014, Kelly and Susan were attending the Teach Every Nation conference in South Africa led by their friend Dr. Bruce Wilkinson. The couple had come to the conference for a rich time in the Word of God and to support pastors that had come from the countries of southern Africa. They were enjoying a time of corporate praise and worship, and in that moment Kelly said Ireland was in no way on his mind. That is why he was completely caught off guard when the Holy Spirit reminded him of the verse in Deuteronomy 11:8 he'd been given so many years before: "Observe therefore all the commands I am giving you today, so that you may have the strength to go in and take over the land that you are crossing the Jordan to possess."

The words he heard God speak to him shook him to the core.

"Kelly, I sent you to a land and you went to a city."

In that moment, Kelly came to an instant understanding of how the ministry, within its existing infrastructure, could go beyond Galway, throughout the nation with the school retreat program with the Gospel of Christ. He felt a challenge from the Lord. The current school retreats that An Tobar Nua was running were reaching 1,200 students a year. Why couldn't they reach 12,000 students? Why not 120,000 students a year? Out of the blue, a new dream was dropped into Kelly's heart. He could envision, at that moment, how the students in far-removed areas of Ireland might be reached with the message of Christ they had been giving in Galway for the last two decades. Now, preparations are already underway to bring that vision to pass.

In the last thirty years Ireland has transformed faster than imaginable. This once primarily agrarian nation is now considered the Silicon Valley of Europe. A people that were once considered backwater are now world leaders in music, education, tourism, film, finance, and charity endeavors. But as Ireland's stock has grown in the eyes of the world, her spirituality has waned. Ireland is on a crash course as a full-blown secular society. But deep in the collective consciousness of the Irish is a rich heritage filled with saints and scholars from an age long past. This is a unique moment in Irish history where a small window of opportunity remains for the Irish to be reminded of their Christian roots and rekindled into the faith of their mothers and fathers who were compelled by the Holy Spirit to bring the Good News of Jesus to the edges of the known world. As author Thomas Cahill once wrote, "And that's how the Irish saved civilization."

The story of An Tobar Nua, in the words of its founders Kelly and Susan Curry, is the story of ordinary people, invited to a fantastic call under the extraordinary guidance of an extraordinary God. In the coming years, the staff at An Tobar Nua looks out unto the horizon, like the Irish monks of the past, to say, "Take us where You will, O God. We are Your children and we long to do Your will."

Afterword

WE HUNG A PLAQUE ON THE WALL in An Tobar Nua that says, "God writes straight with crooked lines." We jokingly say it is the story of that old building, whose walls, floors and ceilings all seemed to be at crooked angles as they'd settled throughout the years. Lovingly restored, those crooked lines are now incorporated into the final structure, beautifully embraced. And so it is with us. God takes crooked people, bent toward everything but He who made us, and writes our lives in straight lines that can spell out His purpose.

~

We are two ordinary crooked people who came in contact with an extraordinary God, whose touch has made all the difference in our lives and changed them from what they might have been. This contact started us on the most exciting journey—beyond what we ever could have asked or imagined—and our Guide was the ultimate in navigating the paths we travelled. Anything good that is noticeable in our spiritual walk can be found in those places where we've been conformed to Christ's image, to mirror His beauty.

Though we've often openly and willingly shared our story—God's story of radically changing two people in much need of His grace—it's been far more difficult to see it put to paper. It's a prospect we didn't look for and didn't want. However, repeatedly throughout the years, we've been asked to write down the steps that led to 25/27 Lower

Dominick Street and to tell the stories of that old beautiful building and how it came to be. Our approach would have been to tell the story of An Tobar Nua. Yet Shawn, the master storyteller, thought otherwise and we yielded, asking him to tell more stories than simply our own. Thank you, Shawn, for your patience, love and even more patience as we worked through this process.

We are the least of those He has used and our story is woven in with the stories of so many amazing people that have surrendered to Jesus and allowed Him to shape their lives. Many parts of this account are just puzzle pieces to the bigger picture He is laying out in Galway and all of Ireland. To be intertwined in what Jesus is doing in and with others as He works in and with us still leaves us awe-struck by His grace. God has scattered our hearts throughout the world through the many precious people we've encountered and loved on this journey. To them we are indebted and we pray that we have touched their lives as they have touched ours. What a joy it is to be serving Christ with His scattered and yet unified body, His people, His church.

We are thankful for the deposit of the Word of God into our hearts by so many people, especially Susan's mom, Betty, who spoke it and lived it for us to see. Also, for Pastor Jim Holbrook, and for Chris Thomas and the teachers of Ravencrest who rooted us deeper, as did Bruce Wilkinson, who challenged us onward.

We give our love and gratitude to two special couples who have journeyed with us from the day we formed FICM in the U.S., Dave and Shirley Moreland and Raymond and Holly Johnson. Thank you for the backbone you have been for us. We are thankful for our Irish board, Patrick Keane, Dr. Joe FitzGibbon and Gerardine Weir, and for past board members, Pat Cregg and Mike Shortt. Thank you for standing with us and grounding us on Irish soil.

We are so grateful for our families who have stood with us as we traveled this road. It's meant many times of being away when we dearly wanted to be with you. Thank you for your love and prayers. We are especially blessed by our daughters, Natalie and Leah, who weren't called as we were, but who allowed Ireland to become their story. In many ways they belong more to Ireland than we do. It would have been a lonely journey without you both. We treasure your open hearts.

Finally, how could we ever name all of the people who are part of An Tobar Nua—all of the lives that have worked in unison to see the Work of God take precedent over individual plans? Their input and wisdom has helped to shape the direction of An Tobar Nua and the vision of sharing of Christ's love. We have sampled some of their stories in these pages but there are so many others that could be told. The individuals and stories are factual, though some names are omitted. In telling this story, we have tried to relay it accurately, but we recognize the challenge that perspective and perception play in recall. No harm or criticism is meant toward any individual or group. We have the utmost respect for the body of Christ in Ireland, and great love for all her people. We trust the details will stand on their own. To all of you, we are forever thankful and we fully recognize that each of you have been a gift and blessing of God to our lives.

We can only pray that as your read you'll be pointed to the very One who made it happen. Without Jesus, none of this would have been accomplished. He is the main character of this story and He is the One we pray will be revealed in all His glory. One of our Bible school teachers from Ravencrest, Bonnie Thomas, often said, "God is behind all the scenes and He is moving all the scenes that He is behind." We have found that to be true. He is a great God and the stories He wants to write with each of our lives are beyond what we could write on our own. And the end—to be with Christ forever—is the "Happily Ever After" that we pray each of you will know by first finding yourself in relationship with Christ Jesus.

—Kelly and Susan Curry

By faith Abraham, when he was called to go out into a place which he should after receive for an inheritance, obeyed; and he went out, not knowing whither he went.
Hebrews 11:8

Whither he went, he knew not; it was enough for him to know that he went with God. He leant not so much upon the promises as upon the Promiser. He looked not on the difficulties of his lot, but on the King, eternal, immortal, invisible, the only wise God, who had deigned to appoint his course, and would certainly vindicate Himself.
O glorious faith! This is thy work, these are thy possibilities; contentment to sail with sealed orders, because of unwavering confidence in the love and wisdom of the Lord High Admiral; willinghood to rise up, leave all, and follow Christ, because of the glad assurance that earth's best cannot bear comparison with Heaven's least.
—F. B. Meyer

An Tobar Nua is an Irish & American café/coffeeshop, one street away from the historic Claddagh, overlooking the canal in the popular Westend of Galway, Ireland on 25/27 Lower Dominick Street.

Drop in we would love to meet you, or visit our foundation website *www.foundationinchrist.org* to learn more about our ministry.

The café website is
https://antobarnua.com